Walks wi[th]
in
Yorkshi[re]

WENSLEYDALE

Mary Welsh

A **QUESTA**Guide

© Mary Welsh 2005

ISBN 1 898808 22 8

Published by
Questa Publishing Ltd., PO Box 520, Bamber Bridge, Preston, Lancashire PR5 8LF
and printed by
Carnmor Print, 95/97 London Road, Preston, Lancashire PR1 4BA

Contents

Introduction

Wensleydale

For young people walking through Wensleydale for the first time is spellbinding. It is a region to which you can always return and recapture that first wonderful feeling. Wensleydale is part of the Yorkshire Dales National Park and footpaths take you through glorious hay meadows and deciduous woodland. Tracks lead you over wild moorland, the haunt of curlew, golden plover, snipe and skylark. In this book there are some steepish climbs to please the more adventurous, and gentle strolls beside the River Ure for those seeking quietness and beauty.

Wensleydale is full of contrasts. Towards Leyburn the valley spreads wide. Meadows are larger and there are fine trees creating an air of gracious parkland. Nearer the head of the dale, the limestone hills provide a wonderful foil for the bright green fields but do not overshadow them. Cotter End, Wether Fell, Addlebrough and Penhill stand back, stepped and terraced overlooking the River Ure. Towards Aysgarth the river continues its journey by descending in dramatic waterfalls. Its tributaries, Cotter, Widdale, Hardraw, Gayle, Baine and Apedale, drop down in great exuberance to join the Ure.

It is a dale full of history. At Bainbridge it has a Roman road and the site of a fort; near Caperby, West Burton and Castle Bolton are pre-Conquest and medieval lynchets, grassy terraces once ploughed by oxen; Middleham has motte and bailey earthworks, predating the remains of its castle; Bolton Castle, started in 1379, dominates the land around, and was Mary, Queen of Scots' prison; the ruins of Jervaulx and Coverham abbeys are havens of peace; Nappa Hall is a fortified manor house, the battlemented towers of which provided protection in the turbulent 15th century; Countersett was a focal point for Quakers.

Wensleydale has fine churches to visit. It has many villages with a wealth of gracious houses, cottages and other small dwellings grouped round a central green, where in the past cattle could be corralled at night for safety. Other villages are built on a linear plan, with the green towards one end. In 1202, Wensley was granted its market charter. It became very important and gave its name to the dale. But in the 16th century, it was devastated by the plague and its trade went to Leyburn, set on a hill with shops all round its spacious square. Delightful, too, is the market town in the upper dale, Hawes, a bustling cheerful place from which roads radiate in all directions.

An important industry in the dale was lead mining, and villages, like Preston-under-Scar and West Witton, were built to house miners. Close by was Keld Head mine and Cobscar mine, which were dug into a lead-yielding belt of land that stretched across Wensleydale into Swaledale.

The footpaths that criss-cross the dale make for ideal walking. Start with the shorter walks and gradually work up to the more demanding ones when youngsters, for whom this book is compiled, are ready to tackle them. All the walks have interesting places to visit and young people will spot even more than are mentioned here. The views are magnificent. The wildlife reflects the soil and rock below. History, tragedy and comedy seem all about the dale. A gentle introduction to hill walking in such a glorious area will set children off on what could become a compulsive, lifelong and extremely healthy pastime.

1
Lady Anne's Highway and the rise of the River Ure

The River Ure rises on the wild moorland of Ure Head. It trickles steadily, descends as a stream, hides for a short distance underground, and crosses Lady Anne's Highway. This pleasingly-named track forms the spine of this delightful walk, which takes in a diminutive church, comes close to the Carlisle-Settle railway, and crosses Hell Gill. Young people should approach the latter with care.

Start: A lay-by south of Shotlock Tunnel on the B6259 (GR788943)

Total distance: 7.4km (4½ miles)

Height gain: 66m (217 feet)

Difficulty: Easy walking all the way. Steepish climb above the church

1 From the lay-by on the B-road, walk south to pass the western corner of Lunds Wood. Continue on to take a signposted stile on the left. Walk diagonally left to cross pleasing walled pastures by three stone step-stiles. Then straddle another stile into a cleared area at the edge of the wood. Bear right and the then follow the indistinct path, keeping on the same diagonal (north-east) through the conifers, an unusual pleasure because the trees have been brashed and you can walk upright – but it is dark. The way is occasionally marked with yellow arrows on the trees and three footbridges take you across little streams. In 300m you reach the access track through the wood, where you turn right.

2 Cross the River Ure on a sturdy footbridge and a short distance beyond, go through a gate in the wall, on the right, to visit the little graveyard and the church, which is locked.

The tiny church was built in the early 18th-century. It served a very scattered parish. The gravestones, heavily encrusted with lichen, commemorate local people, the

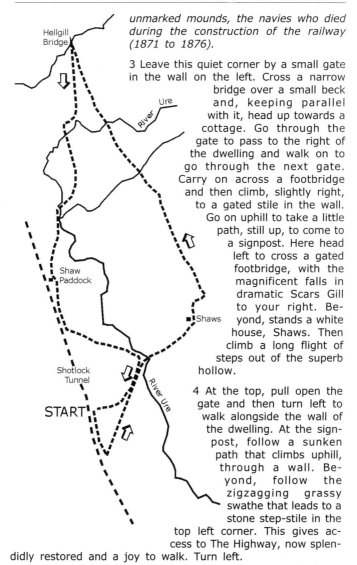

unmarked mounds, the navies who died during the construction of the railway (1871 to 1876).

3 Leave this quiet corner by a small gate in the wall on the left. Cross a narrow bridge over a small beck and, keeping parallel with it, head up towards a cottage. Go through the gate to pass to the right of the dwelling and walk on to go through the next gate. Carry on across a footbridge and then climb, slightly right, to a gated stile in the wall. Go on uphill to take a little path, still up, to come to a signpost. Here head left to cross a gated footbridge, with the magnificent falls in dramatic Scars Gill to your right. Beyond, stands a white house, Shaws. Then climb a long flight of steps out of the superb hollow.

4 At the top, pull open the gate and then turn left to walk alongside the wall of the dwelling. At the signpost, follow a sunken path that climbs uphill, through a wall. Beyond, follow the zigzagging grassy swathe that leads to a stone step-stile in the top left corner. This gives access to The Highway, now splendidly restored and a joy to walk. Turn left.

The Highway is named after the 17th-century Lady Anne

Clifford, who inherited the castles of Appleby, Brough, Brougham, Skipton and Pendragon. After repairing and rebuilding the castles she spent the latter part of her life visiting them, driving along the old road in her four-wheeled carriage, and caring for the needs of her tenants.

5 Step out along the track, past the ruins of the aptly-named High Hall, which stands just before Washer Gill. Ford the small beck and take the lower track. Cross another small stream and then walk on to step across the young River Ure as it comes chuckling out of its grassy, lonely gill on your right.

6 The track then sweeps on towards Hell Gill, and crosses it by Hell Gill Bridge. The bridge has high parapets and if children want to peep over to see the enormous depth of the gill, they must be held tightly. Through the incredible limestone gorge hurries the River Eden, which soon turns northwards and into Cumbria.

The Highway was once so busy with travellers that it attracted highwaymen. One, nicknamed 'Swift Nick', was reputed to have leapt across Hell Gill on his grey horse on his way to the inn at High Dyke. A cottage attached to the inn was once Lunds School.

7 After a pause here, turn round and walk back a short distance, to take a wide grassy swathe, descending right. Look for the well preserved limekiln on your left and then, a few steps along, you can see the young Ure, passing through the wall of The Highway and descending through ash trees before dropping down over several limestone outcrops. Descend steadily to cross Green Bridge, a tractor crossing over the sweetly singing Ure. Carry on with Ure Crook curving away to your right.

8 Follow the good track to eventually cross How Beck Bridge, over the now wider Ure. Stroll on to Shore Paddock farm, where the track joins the B-road. Turn left and walk on parallel with the railway line for 450m. Then take the signposted stile on the left. Head half-right to climb a little eminence. Here pick up a tractor path coming from a gate on the road. Head on in the same direction to cross a footbridge over the Ure at the lower edge of Lunds Wood. Go through a gap-stile on the right and walk alongside the river. Step across the small beck and then cross the footbridge taken at the start of the walk. Go on ahead up the track to the road.

Along the Way

The River Ure springs on Ure Head (Sails 666m), an area much wilder and more lonely that the countryside it meanders through by the time it has reached Hawes. From this small market town it flows steadily, through meadows, for mile after mile. Villages lie close to it, or sit on terraces above it. Near Aysgarth the Ure changes character and descends exuberantly, for 60m, over great ledges of limestone in three sets of impressive falls, before surging on. At Myton-on-Swale, the Ure joins the Swale to become the River Ouse, which in turn flows into the Humber Estuary and the North Sea.

The B6259 from the Moorcock Inn to Shaw Paddock was constructed in 1825, replacing The Highway. The track through the conifers to Lunds Church and the footbridge over the Ure were constructed by Mr Scott Macfie who lived at Shaws, the house passed high on the slopes. The track and the bridge made the church more accessible and saved parishioners from fording the Ure.

Lunds Church

But for its bell-cote Lunds Church might be mistaken for a barn. In 1839 the rain and snow poured through a hole in the roof and the bell became broken. The poor sexton had to call the faithful by climbing up and shouting through the hole in a way that he thought sounded like the bell. The church, once the focus for the valley, was probably built early in the eighteenth century. It was constructed of rough stone by the local people and it has blended well with the surrounding countryside ever since. Lunds never kept its vicars or curates for very long. They regarded a couple of years spent at the church as a way of getting promotion to a higher office. In twenty-eight years Lunds had thirteen incumbents.

2
Hawes to Hardraw

Walking from Hawes to Hardraw, visiting the lovely hill hamlets of Sedbusk and Simonstone, is a delightful way of introducing young people to the pleasures of Wensleydale. The walk has many paved trods to traverse, numerous squeeze stiles to pass through, a magnificent waterfall to view, and a pleasing road bridge and a gem of a packhorse bridge to cross. The walk starts and ends at Hawes, often called T'Haas after its original name The Hawes. The charming market town sits at the head of Wensleydale and has many interesting shops to visit. The whole family will enjoy a free visit to the ropeworks to see a ropewalk. It is situated in the station car park.

Start: Pay-and-display car park at the old Hawes railway station (GR876898)

Total distance: 6km (4miles)

Height gain: 60m (197 feet)

Difficulty: Easy: a very satisfactory walk, full of interest and a real family favourite

1 Leave the car park by the back left corner and climb the slope, acutely left, leading up to Brunt Acres Road. Cross with care and walk right to pass Hawes Business Park. Just beyond, go through the kissing-gate onto a delightful paved trod, signposted the 'Pennine Way'. Continue to the end of the flagged way to go through a gate.

These flagged paths, firmly embedded in the ground, would have been used by lead miners, coal miners and quarrymen. They led to limekilns. They have also been used by generations of walkers and have prevented the grass from becoming worn on either side.

2 Cross the road, and take a step right to go through a gap-stile in the wall. Beyond walk a narrow path, with the surging River Ure to your right. At the path end, rejoin the road and cross the twin-arched Haylands Bridge, built in 1820 over the wide river. Look here for flood holes in the base of the walls, on either side of the river. When the Ure is in spate and it spills over its banks the floodwater runs away through the holes, breaking the force of the water.

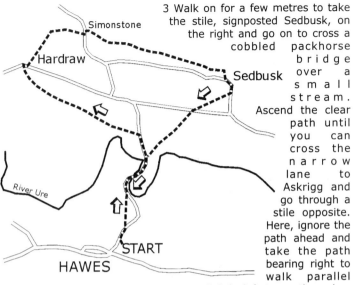

3 Walk on for a few metres to take the stile, signposted Sedbusk, on the right and go on to cross a cobbled packhorse bridge over a small stream. Ascend the clear path until you can cross the narrow lane to Askrigg and go through a stile opposite. Here, ignore the path ahead and take the path bearing right to walk parallel with the wall on your right. Bear slightly left to go through a gated stile and continue in the same general direction to join the minor road to Sedbusk, where you turn left and then right into the small hamlet.

Sedbusk is a small village of sturdy gritstone houses, which sits on a ridge below Abbotside Common. Shutt Lane, climbing out of the village, led to limekilns, quarries and lead mines.

4 Walk beside the tiny village green and, half way along, cross it, left, on a signposted path to pass through two gates, between houses, onto the glorious walled pastures, high above Hawes. From now on the level way continues westwards (ahead). The narrow, mainly paved path crosses seventeen narrow very green pastures.

Each wall is crossed by an easy gated stile two little steps up to a small gate (on a strong spring) and two little steps down. Children will enjoy passing through the stiles and counting them as they go. From this fine path there are spectacular views over the wide dale of Wensley to Wether Fell and one of its buttresses, Yorburgh.

11

5 After a ladder-stile, pass some farm buildings to your left, and go on to a stile onto the minor road, through Simonstone. Turn left and almost immediately, right, to walk the signposted access track to Simonstone Hall, a charming country house, which was once the shooting lodge of the Earl of Wharncliffe.

6 Opposite the main gate, take the gated step-stile on your left and walk right, with the wall to your right, to go through another gated stile. Walk ahead to pass between West House farm on the left and its outbuildings on the right. Beyond the gate or stile, beside the house, bear left to pick up a row of well-mellowed steps, leading down the steep slope to a stile. Beyond more steps, continue to the valley where a flagged path leads through two gates to the road at Hardraw.

7 Turn right into The Green Dragon inn, the only approach to Hardraw Force. Pay your admission, £2 at the time of writing, and walk the good path, beside Fossdale Beck to see the magnificent waterfall, a 30m/96ft single drop, the highest unbroken fall in England. Here you are asked to be responsible for your own safety and not to walk behind the waterfall. Adventurous children should follow their parents' advice. The landowners have put in new paths and a bridge and, at the time of writing, are establishing some extensive paths above and around the glorious scar. There are picnic tables and seats from where you can enjoy the turbulent beck.

8 Return to the main street, cross and take a Pennine Way signposted gate to the right of a modern house. Beyond the gate, turn left to walk the flagged way, passing through more squeeze stiles. Where the flags cease, carry on ahead along a wide grassy, gated swathe, to reach Brunt Acres Road, just above a belt of sycamores. Turn right and follow your outward route back to Hawes.

Along the Way

Hardraw Force is Wensleydale's spectacular attraction. Fossdale Beck descends over Hardraw Scar. The lip is limestone of the Yoredale series and below this, sandstone. The deep plunge pool is backed by shale and the force of the water has eaten away this softer rock, forming caves. Over the years the water of the beck steadily erodes the lip. In 1899 a great storm over Shunner Fell, above, sent a tremendous flood down the ravine and washed away the lip. An artificial one was put in its place by the workmen of the Earl of Wharncliffe.

To the left of the path to the waterfall stands the Church of St Mary and St John, rebuilt in 1880 by the earl. It was often featured in the TV series *All Creatures Great and Small.*

Between the church and the force, inside the grounds of the inn, is a walled enclosure. Here brass band concerts take place and the amphitheatre of rock provides superb acoustics.

Brass bands

In the north of England, brass bands were a feature of life at the beginning of the 19th century, and many villages had their own bands. A brass band contest was held at Hardraw until the 1899 great storm swept away the site. In 1920, part of the original area was rebuilt and contests held until 1926. In recent years a great revival of interest ensures that contests are now held annually.

Walls

The walls of Wensleydale were built to enclose grazing land. Today access through them is by gap-stiles and gated stiles, or by step-stiles and ladder-stiles over them. The fine field barns, one for two or three fields, were used to store hay and house the cattle during the winter. The cows spent the summer in the meadows and then towards winter they were moved into barns. Twice a day the farmer would visit all his barns to feed the cattle from the stored hay and to milk them.

Hawes

Hawes is a lively small town with a bustling market. As Christmas approaches its shops are gaily decorated, the streets hung with lights. Its church, built in 1850, stands high above the main street. Houses cluster close up to it and as you look down on the town, from the hills, it seems a cosy place to live and work. No record of Hawes exists before 1307 but, as trade developed, its position made it a crossing point for packhorse carriers and drovers from the west of the Pennines, and the town achieved a market charter in 1700. In 1877 when the railway connected the town to Leyburn and to the Settle-Carlisle line its prosperity was assured and has continued to do so.

3
Askrigg to Bainbridge and Worton

The limestone fells slope back from the lovely Dales town of Askrigg and quiet walled pastures, many with a traditional barn, creep up to its outskirts. Tall brownstone houses line its main street and many neat cottages, closely packed, edge the winding lanes and ginnels. The fine 17th- and 18th-century houses reflect its days of glory when Askrigg was the chief town in Upper Wensleydale. However in 1725, nearby Hawes won a lawsuit for the right to hold a market, and business slowly drained away from the town. Later this effect was compounded by the A-road that was constructed through Hawes by-passing Askrigg. All the family will enjoy exploring the little town.

Start: St Oswald's church Askrigg (GR948910)
Total distance: 9km (5½ miles)
Height gain: 110m (420 feet)
Difficulty: Generally easy walking all the way

Before you leave the market square, visit the large late-Perpendicular church, the 'Cathedral of Wensleydale', which dates from about 1450. Enjoy the splendid wooden-beamed ceiling of its nave and its fine glass windows. Spend time looking at the lichen-encrusted gravestones, engraved with names and occupations. Many of those remembered were clockmakers, because Askrigg was renowned for its hand-made clocks. A clock maker lacking a tool would design and fashion it to do the job.

1 Leave the cobbled parking area outside the church and bear left along its wall, following the signpost directions for Mill Gill Force. Walk the lane and then, after a few steps along the on-going track, leave it right by a paved way across a buttercup meadow. Continue through a small gate to the right of a disused corn mill, which once generated electricity for Askrigg. Bear right beside the beck that provided power for the mill, and then cross the stiled footbridge and steps into a pasture. Stroll right and in a few paces go through a small gate into glorious woodland.

2 Follow the path beside the boundary wall as it climbs steadily high above the beck. Continue where the path curves right to a signpost. Here take the right branch, which drops gently through trees into a sheer-sided ravine. Ahead lies the magnificent Mill Gill Force descending through a deep narrow cleft in the huge amphitheatre of rock.

3 Return to the signpost and take the upper path through woodland and then on along the stiled way through pastures, still within earshot of the beck. Climb a gap-stile in the wall on your right and ascend left along a path through more woodland. Leave by an arrowed gap-stile on the left, and turn right to come nearer to the beck and a step-stile under a fine ash

tree. Just beyond stands a signpost. This lovely sheltered hollow is where you might wish to take your first break.

4 From the signpost, climb left (bridleway to Helm) up a grassy track to the corner of two walls. Go ahead across a pasture to

pass through a signposted gateless gap. Bear left and follow a path downhill, which eventually becomes a track and keeps parallel with the wall on the left. Continue to a gate to pass in front of the dwellings at Helm (pronounced Hellum). Join a track, wind left and walk on to bear left to descend Skelgill Lane. Just before you reach the B-road to Askrigg, look over the wall, on the right, to see a fine fall on Grange Beck and then, lower, the wide turf bridge over the beck, believed to have been constructed by monks.

5 At Bow Bridge walk left and take, 50m beyond the last dwelling, a stile on the right. Stroll the barely visible flagged path, right. Pass beside the remains of an old chapel, houses and outbuildings and go through stiles. Gap-stiles take you across a private track and then over a superb packhorse bridge, above which was the site of Fors Abbey.

6 Turn left and pass between the abutments of a bridge, part of the now defunct Wensleydale railway. Beyond, walk right along the continuing paved footpath. When the flags cease, carry on in the same general direction to take a gate tucked into the far left corner, which gives access to the road.

7 Stroll left to cross Yore Bridge over the River Ure and go on into the delightful village of Bainbridge. Continue ahead over the greens and follow the A-road as it winds east over Bain Bridge. Pause on the right side of bridge, if the traffic is light (there is no pavement), to see the spectacular cascades on the short river.

8 Stride on, passing on the other side of the road, Brough Hill, the site of a fort occupied by the Romans for 300 years. Take the first right turn, signposted Semerwater, and then climb the gated stile on the left. Strike up the pasture to take a gated stile through the wall on your left. Climb on up to a stile at the top of Brough Scar, with the signpost seen clearly above. Here head left along the delightful wooded scar. Ignore the first signpost and then, after three-quarters of a mile along the lovely way, when you reach the second, take the right branch, signposted Cubeck, out of the trees.

9 Walk uphill to a gate on the left and go on the arrowed gated way. By a telegraph pole an arrow directs you to the far right corner. Pass to the right of the farmhouse and continue ahead to a narrow lane. Turn left and descend the pleasing way to Worton. Cross the A-road, with care, and go through the quiet

hamlet, still descending, to a road bridge across the Ure. Beyond, go through the signposted gate to walk the flagged path, heading for Askrigg Church. When the flags cease go on along the distinct path to climb steps to a stile.

10 Bear left and go through a stranded iron kissing gate. Walk left along the bed of the old railway line, then leave it by steps to climb a good path up a slope to pass through a gate. Carry on to pass through a small gate beside a farm gate. Then wind left to walk a narrow road lined with delightful houses. This brings you to centre of the village and the cobbled parking area.

Along the Way

Fors Abbey: Peter de Quincey, a monk from Brittany, wanted to form a Cistercian Abbey. He chose a site above the packhorse bridge at Grange. Fors Abbey was the first in Wensleydale. It survived for about eleven years in spite of the exposed position, difficult terrain, attacks by wolves and plunder by local people. It was then transferred to friendlier pastures near East Witton and became Jervaulx Abbey. The nearby disused railway was cut through the burial ground and many bones were found.

Askrigg

Askrigg was on the edge of land designated by the Normans as hunting forest. Local people found it a good place to exchange goods, but it was not until 1587 that it received its market charter. This lapsed when Hawes became the rail-head. The television series *All Creatures Great and Small* was filmed in Wensleydale. The real name of the author and vet 'James Herriot' was James Alfred White, and his real veterinary practice was in Thirsk. It was too difficult to change modern day Thirsk into Darrowby of the books and set in the 1930s-40s. Askrigg, with its 17th- and 18th-century houses built of warm, brown stone, packed tightly along the winding main street, was chosen as the location. 'Cringley House' found on a corner near the market cross, was the vets Skeldale House while the King's Arms Hotel became the Drovers' Arms.

4
Bainbridge to Semerwater

This exhilarating walk providing delightful views and lots of historical interest, is centred on the picturesque village of Bainbridge, once an important Roman garrison. Troops occupied its fort on Brough Hill for 300 years. In the first century AD, Emperor Agricola built a road leading west from the village over Wether Fell and on to Ribblehead. Today an easy-to-walk track, known as Cam High Road, follows the course of the original Roman road.

Below the village of Countersett stands Semerwater, a tranquil lake, tree-fringed and lying in a lovely hollow in the hills. On its shore can be seen some large boulders, 'erratics', having been carried from Shap in Cumbria by a glacier and deposited here at the end of the last Ice Age.

Start: On the upper road on the west side of Bainbridge's village green (GR934903)

Total distance: 8km (5 miles)

Height gain: 220m (750 feet)

Difficulty: Generally easy. Steady climb to Hawes End and over Bracken Fell. Numerous narrow gap-stiles overweight dogs will find some of these a problem

1 Ascend the slope to take the signposted fenced path to the left of the primary school. Follow it as it winds right, and then take the waymarked stile, on the left, into a pasture. Stride ahead to take a gated stile opposite. Continue on the stiled way to pass a fine house on the right. Go through the next stile and then walk ahead to pass through the next one to the right of a lean-to. Carry on to pass through a gateless gap to the left of a barn. Stroll on to climb a gated stile in the far right corner of the next pasture, close to an electricity pole.

2 Keep beside a wall and just before a stream, Goodman Syke, walk left beside it and follow the hurrying water to a signpost. Here cross a plank bridge, over the stream, and go through a stile in the wall ahead. Bear left through a gateless gap and continue on to walk in front of a house, Greensley Bank. Wind

round left of the end of the house to take a gate. Descend left to take a gated stile in the wall on your left. Follow the way mark directing you uphill, bearing diagonally up the large pasture on an indistinct path to the top right corner. Beyond the gap in the wall take the stile, just along on the right, onto Cam High Road, where you turn right.

3 Stride the Roman road, which stretches ahead for as far as you can see. From this gradually ascending airy track notice the pleasing field patterns created by sturdy walls, many pastures complete with their own characteristic barns. At any minute you feel you might meet a Roman troop matching fast along the way.

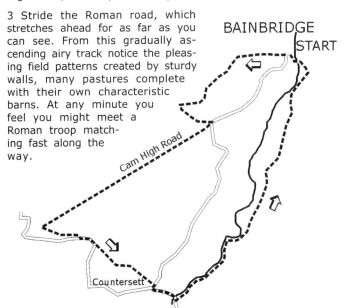

BAINBRIDGE

START

Cam High Road

Countersett

4 Three hundred metres before you reach the road ahead, take the easy-to-miss gated stile through the wall on your left. Walk half-left through the rushes and then continue on the same diagonal up and up on a fairly distinct path to take a gap-stile onto the fell road to Countersett, below the imposing side of Crag Hill.

5 Walk left for a few steps and then pass through the signposted gate on the left. Beyond, drop downhill (right) for a short distance to go through a gap-stile. Then descend a delightful grassy gully, with the whole of Semerwater coming into view. At the end of the gully, follow a grassy swathe across the pasture (left), keeping below a small fenced enclosure, to a gap-stile.

19

6 Turn right and continue down parallel with the wall on your right and a tumbledown barn to your left. Go on descending to cross a stream and pass through the awkward gate ahead. Drop down the grassy slope to come to a fence. Walk right along side it to a gate on to a lane. Turn right to reach a signpost. Here turn left to walk a few steps to see gracious Countersett Hall, the meeting house, and the old school. Return to the signpost and follow the directions for Stalling Busk. Then, after enjoying another superb view of the lake and a pause on the well placed seats, descend the left fork to cross the charming three-arched Semerwater Bridge.

7 To see the group of Shap granite boulders near the water's edge walk on. These are known as the Carlow Stone (see walk 5) and the Mermaids Stones.

8 Return towards the bridge and take the stile, now on your right, before it (signposted: 'Bainbridge: 2 miles'). The walk goes ahead beside the pretty stream which unites with River Ure in less than two miles and which is often described as Yorkshire's shortest river. Walk on along the stiled way beside the Bain. Then continue round a large meander, cross a little footbridge, climb a stile and then a ladder-stile.

9 From here after a little boulder-hopping over a wet area, climb a wide grassy way up onto Bracken Hill, with superb views in all directions. Then begin your gradual descent on fine grassy trods towards Bainbridge. Ignore the stile away to your right onto the Blean Lane. Remain on the trods all the way to the stile on to the A684. Turn left and walk into the village, pausing, with care, on the bridge to look upstream to see the fine cascades on the Bain as it rages on it way to join the Ure.

Along the Way

Semerwater: Although Semerwater owes its existence to the Ice Age, legend tells another story about its formation.

Once a beautiful city stood where the water now lies. An angel visited it disguised as a beggar. At each house he asked for food but was roughly turned away, except at a mean cottage outside the city. Here a poor man and his wife took him in and fed him. Next day a terrible noise was heard and the city sank and was covered with water, all except the tiny cottage.

5
Addlebrough

*This walk starts from the pretty village of Thornton Rust, which
sits on densely birch-clad Thornton Scar. It overlooks Wensleydale's flat pastures on either side of the happily meandering
River Ure. Behind the village the fells climb up and these are
crossed, in a south-west direction, on good grassy tracks and
paths to the summit of lofty Addelbrough. From here there is a
wonderful view and all the family will enjoy looking up and down
almost the whole of Wensleydale. Below the summit nestles
Bainbridge and Worton and across the dale, behind Askrigg,
flares the lovely scar of Ellerkin. The start of the waymarked
descent is fairly steep but is one that children will enjoy.*

Start: Well-signed free parking area in Thornton Rust, along
a track, on the south side of the old road as it passes through
the village.

Total distance: 7.4km (4½ miles)

Height gain: 210m (670 feet)

Difficulty: A gentle climb until you reach the foot of
Addlebrough and even then children will enjoy the climb up.
An exhilarating and almost dry underfoot-walk

1 From the parking track, cross the little ford and carry on up
the lovely walled track, the left of two. Ignore the footpath off
left and later a track off left and follow the rising walled track
as it bears right. Where the wall on the left, turns left, leave the
track and take the signposted bridleway, also on the left. which
soon becomes a lovely wide grassy swathe sweeping across
the rough pasture, bearing slightly right to a gate.

2 Beyond, the ground is marked by short tracks marked by a
tractor. Here walk a couple of steps right and then pick up the
track, just slightly to the left, which continues in the same
general direction over the huge pasture. Half way over there
are several little streams to cross and the track can be muddy.
Here the youngsters can choose the driest way for the family.
The way soon improves and at a Y-junction of tracks, take the
right branch to reach a ladder-stile over the wall.

3 Once over, you are on National Trust limited access land.
Walk ahead, along a permissive path to a white-topped

waymarked post. This directs you, right, to a ladder-stile over another wall. Then walk ahead on a distinct path, parallel with a wall to your left. Where this wall turns left before it climbs up the slopes of Addlebrough, carry on the path, ahead, to the next white-topped post. This directs you on a narrow path up the steepish slope. It soon branches and you need to take the

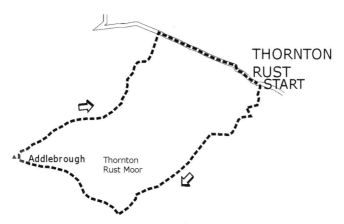

right fork. This climbs steadily, goes over a hillock and then leads over the rough pasture (where you might see golden plover) to a stile over another wall. Just beyond is the summit cairn. You may wish to spend a little time here. If so children should be under control and be reminded not to go too near to he edge of the scar.

4 Then go on from the cairn to the next white-topped post, which directs you down a path through a gully in the outcropping scar. Follow the steepish path as it winds down and down to come close to the wall on your right. Walk on to cross duck-boarding which takes you across a stream to the next ladder-stile which you climb.

5 Carry on along the clear path that brings you to a stile over a fence. Beyond, turn left and then cross diagonally to a ladder-stile (beyond a gate) into the next pasture. Just to your right is a delightful limestone dry gill, where scattered rowans grace its banks. Go through the next wall by a gateless gap to walk a farm track. Where it swings left to a farm, follow the white-topped post that directs you, right, to a stile over a fence, under a rowan on the edge of the gill.

6 Walk on down, now with a wall to your right and soon climb the ladder-stile over it. Turn left and descend beside the wall on the left. Go over the next ladder-stile. Walk on beside the wall on your left to reach two stiles, close together that give access to the road on Thornton Scar. Bear right to walk the quiet way to Thornton

Along the Way

Each Wensleydale hill shows a different face to the vale below, though most end, pleasingly, in a series of terraces, where the softer layers of rock have been worn away. As you start at the head of the dale you pass Cotter End, Widdale Fell, Wether Fell, Addleborough, Penhill and Witton Fell. A legend linking this walk with the Semerwater walk is that a giant hurled a stone from the top of Addlebrough at the devil on Crag Hill (walked around on the way down to the lake). It fell short and is one of the boulders seen beside the lake. The devil hurled one back and this fell just short of Addlebrough's summit. It is called the Devil's Stone on maps.

Golden plover

A golden plover has sharply pointed, angled wings and rapid flight. It is a bullet-headed, short-billed bird, with a high forehead. It runs lightly over the pastures. In summer the upper parts of the adult bird are mottled with black and golden-yellow. The under parts of the abdomen and its cheeks are black. It is sometimes known as the 'whistler', as it whistles frequently when on the wing. The normal distinct single note is heard at all seasons. It nests on the upper moorland, bare or clothed with coarse grass, as on the top of Addlebrough. Watch out for it because it is a delight to see.

6
Aysgarth to Bolton Castle

Everyone should visit the splendid Aysgarth Falls. In spate they are magnificent. This walk passes the middle and lower falls, with delightful views across the River Ure to the church. There are pleasing viewing platforms from which the whole family can see the tempestuous river, though you should take good notice of the National Park's advice not to stray from the platforms. The walk then passes over meadows, climbing very gently to the forbidding Bolton Castle, an exciting place for children to visit, with its great towers and castellations. The route then returns you over more pleasing rolling countryside. At the end of the ramble you might like to take a very short stroll to see the splendid upper falls at Aysgarth.

Start: Aysgarth Falls National Park Centre (GR012887)

Total distance: 9.5km/6 miles

Height gain: 120m (390 feet)

Difficulty: Easy walking expect some mud after rain. Steepish climb to the castle. Thoresby Lane can get overgrown in the summer if the council are late cutting back the vegetation.

1 Leave the National Park Centre by the entrance and follow the railed path, right, to the road. Cross with care and go through a gate into Freeholders' Wood. Follow the signpost directing you down steps to the see the superb middle falls. Return to the main path and carry on through the fine woodland. Go past a signpost and continue on to descend a railed way to view the dramatic lower falls.

2 Return back along the good path to the signpost, noted earlier, and take the footpath, now acute right, signposted Castle Bolton and Redmire. Continue on beside a long fence beyond which many trees have been planted in a pasture called The Riddings. At the end of the fence go through a gated stile and follow the signpost, continuing ahead through the peaceful countryside towards Hollins House farm.

3 Go through a gate and follow the track between the buildings,

to join a reinforced track along which you continue for a short distance, watching out for the signpost that directs you away from the track, right. Pass through the left of two gates and carry on to pass through a stile in a wall. Watch out for your first view of Castle Bolton.

4 Descend, in the same general direction, to the next stile, beside a gate and a signpost. Ignore the stile and turn right before the wall. Walk on with the wall to your left. Go over two stiles very close to each other. Stride on a rather wet way, with a wall now to

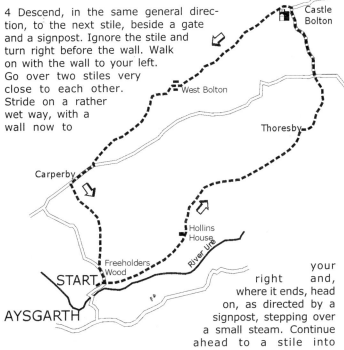

your right and, where it ends, head on, as directed by a signpost, stepping over a small steam. Continue ahead to a stile into Thoresby Lane, a narrow path between fine hedgerows.

5 Carry on along the long, lovely way to arrive at a gate, beyond which lies a metalled road. Pass the buildings of Low Thoresby, on your right. A short distance along, leave the track and take a narrow path left, cross a footbridge over Beldon Beck and climb the step-stile on the left.

6 Bear left to go through a wall gap and turn right to walk a long thin pasture, with the castle looming up ahead. Where the pasture widens stride on to pass through a gated stile and then on to the far left corner to take a stile onto the road to Askrigg. Cross and walk uphill towards the castle. Here children will find

25

this steepish hill tiresome but, hopefully, with the castle towering overhead, it will encourage them on best stop for lots of pauses.

7 After visiting the village, the church and the exciting castle, where you can obtain refreshments if it is open, walk west, with the castle to your left and the church to your right. Where the tarmac ends, go through a gate and then strike diagonally left over the pasture to go through a gated stile at the left end of a tiny wood of sycamores. Walk ahead through the trees to climb the next stile and the follow the signpost direction for Aysgarth.

8 Continue ahead over fine strip lynchets, slightly left, to a gate in a fence. Beyond descend, left, to an arrowed telegraph pole. Here follow the poles along the line of a lynchet to a gated stile ahead. Stroll on a narrow path, which descends to a footbridge over Beldon Beck in its pretty tree-lined gill. Climb right, to a stile in the wall. Carry on beside the yellow-marked fence posts, to your right, to approach the front of West Bolton farm. Wind left round its wall to go through a gate and follow the reinforced track, past outbuildings.

9 Where the track soon winds left, take the gap-stile in the wall, on your right. Climb the slope to the next stile and then carry on to take a stile beside the top corner of the woodland, on your left. Gently descend to cross a stream, on stones and boulders, where it divides into two.

10 Then stride upstream to a gated stile in the wall ahead. Continue on along a clear green swathe, with the wall/fence/ hedge to the right. Go through a gate and carry on, keeping to the right of a barn. Beyond the next gate, join a track, which can be muddy, and descend towards East End farm. At the bottom of the slope and just before the farm buildings, take a waymarked path, left, to a stile to a plank across a stream (all very muddy here) and walk ahead, beside the wall on your left, to go through a signposted gap to the road.

11 Turn right to walk into the village of Caperby. Take the signposted gate, on the left, opposite the Wheatsheaf Inn. Walk ahead to cross a footbridge and continue beside the wall on the right. Go through a wall gap and carry on with the wall to your left to a stile to Low Lane. Cross and take a couple of steps, right, to go through a stile into a pasture.

12 Stroll on with the wall to your right and go through a

signposted gap just before the start of a hedge. Strike diagonally right across a pasture to a stile near to the right corner. Continue on in the same general diagonal, crossing the line of stiles to re-enter Freeholders' Wood. Walk ahead to a track, where you bear right for a couple of steps and then bear off left and stroll on to join the road. Turn left and pass under the railway bridge to return to the National Park Centre.

13 If you wish to visit the lovely upper falls, follow the signpost directions from the car park.

Along the Way

River Ure: The River Ure flows quietly until it reaches Aysgarth, where it descends 50m/200feet by the Aysgarth Falls, to flow through Lower Wensleydale. The underlying layers of shale have been eroded by the river and have undercut the limestone, creating a series of steps in the river bed.

Freeholders' Wood: is managed by the National Park. It is divided into plots, and approximately, every 15 years, in rotation, the trees are cut back to stump level. Once this would have provided timber for fencing, firewood, and laths. Today it provides an ideal habitat for nesting birds.

Bolton Castle: was built in the reign of Richard II by Richard le Scrope. Mary, Queen of Scots, was held prisoner here for six months. In the Civil War, it was held for the king and withstood a lengthy siege, but was captured by the Parliamentarians and dismantled in 1647. Leave time to visit its halls, chambers, monk's cell, armourer's forge, ale house, threshing floor, dungeon and battlements.

Caperby: was a centre of Quakerism and was visited by George Fox on his preaching tours. It is also the 'birthplace' of the breed of sheep known as Wensleydales.

Lynchets: are green terraces of Anglian strip cultivation. These terraces, built up in steps, were wide enough for a plough to be pulled by a team of oxen . They stretched horizontally across the slopes to assist conservation of the soil, where the erosion by rain was considerable.

Finding your way: There are so many signposts, waymarks, yellow blobs, arrows, gated stiles, gap-stiles and step-stiles that children will enjoy seeking them out and finding the way, with the castle in sight for much of the outward route to keep them in the right direction.

7
West Witton

This walk starts at West Witton, a grey, linear village that stretches along either side of A684. More than a century ago, it housed miners who walked to the mines across Bolton Park. The village lies below Penhill, where crags stand up as battlements. Towards the end of this walk the route climbs to the Beacon on the Penhill.

Start: From a lay-by on the south side of the A684. This lies east of West Witton, just before the first (or last) house in the village (GR065886)

Total distance: 12 km (7½ miles)

Height gain: 360m (1175 feet)

Difficulty: Steady ascent onto Caple Bank and Middleham High Moor, where children will enjoy finding the many stiles to be negotiated. The return over Melmerby Moor will give them a taste of wilderness walking. The climb to the Beacon is optional if by this time youngsters are flagging but great fun to have a picnic on the flat part of the hill where the Beacon stands

1 From the lay-by walk on a few steps towards the first house in the village and take the short signposted track on your left. Go through a gate, turn left and follow the signposted way beside the wall to go through a gap-stile. Carry on ahead through a wall gap, a gate and stiles to a muddy track and continue to its end. Turn right to walk a wide tree-lined track, with Park Gate farm to your left.

2 At the end of the track, mainly lined with horse chestnut trees, cross a track and climb a stile ahead. Ascend a steep narrow path through trees to take a stile out of the woodland and then a second stile through a wall.

3 Walk ahead through a pasture to another stile then cross a much wider pasture, still maintaining a straight line to go through a narrow squeeze stile. Continue ahead, uphill, towards woodland, with an arm of trees on either side. Climb the difficult-to-spot stile through the wall between the two arms, and then ascend steps through the trees to go through a gate. Straddle the stile over the wall to cross a narrow road to a stile in the wall opposite.

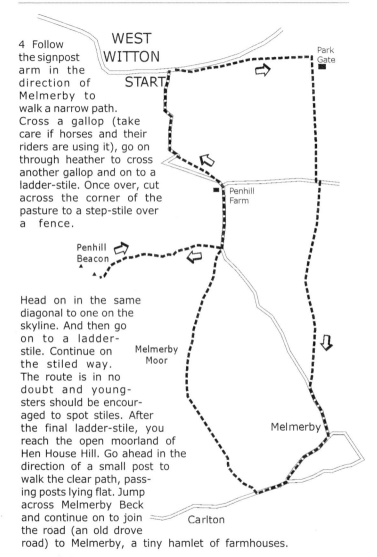

4 Follow the signpost arm in the direction of Melmerby to walk a narrow path. Cross a gallop (take care if horses and their riders are using it), go on through heather to cross another gallop and on to a ladder-stile. Once over, cut across the corner of the pasture to a step-stile over a fence.

Head on in the same diagonal to one on the skyline. And then go on to a ladder-stile. Continue on the stiled way. The route is in no doubt and young-sters should be encour-aged to spot stiles. After the final ladder-stile, you reach the open moorland of Hen House Hill. Go ahead in the direction of a small post to walk the clear path, pass-ing posts lying flat. Jump across Melmerby Beck and continue on to join the road (an old drove road) to Melmerby, a tiny hamlet of farmhouses.

5 Turn left to descend to the T-junction, where there is a small bench seat, just right for a quick break. Then turn right and

walk a quiet lane. As you approach the outskirts of the fine village of Carlton you come beside a pretty stream on your right. Just before it tumbles down from the moorland, look for the signposted gate on the right.

6 Follow a sunken track uphill, with the gill to your left. Keep to the right of a barn. Go through the gate in right corner, with a stile just beyond. Carry on up a large pasture, with Penhill Beacon directly ahead. At the top of the pasture climb a stile into a fenced pasture and walk on to take the gate up against the wall on your right onto Melmerby Moor.

7 Walk ahead, cross a shooters' track and, ignoring the track directly ahead, which leads to a row of grouse butts, take a narrow path going off half-right, the old peat track from Coverdale to West Witton. Just before it joins the Melmerby road, cross another track and go on to a wall corner. Turn left and, a few steps along the road, take the gate on your left (signposted: 'Penhill Beacon'). Walk ahead, on an indistinct way, to pass through a gateless gap to join a glorious, wide grassy trod, which continues through pastures to come to the foot of the beacon. Climb the steep slope to where the edifice once fine, but now a little tumbledown stands on flat-topped Penhill.

8 The hill commands stunning views in all directions and the family will enjoy identifying them. Then descend by the same route and as you go you might spot Sutton Bank and the North Yorkshire Moors. At the road, turn left and descend to a T-junction. Here turn left and take, immediately, a small gate on the right. Follow the clear trod as it descends, steadily winding left with fine views far below of West Witton and Wensleydale. Eventually it rejoins the road through a signposted gate, which stands in a sea of mud - be warned. Turn right and descend to West Witton, where you turn right to return to the parking lay-by.

Along the Way

Penhill Beacon has been used as a signalling site for centuries and was in use during the Napoleonic Wars. It was also fired to celebrate royal occasions.

West Witton once had a Norman Church but the villagers had to bury their dead in Wensley churchyard, unable to fine enough soil in their own until about 1780 when soil was carted in. The present church was built in the 19th century.

8
Leyburn to Wensley

*The village that gives its name to Wensleydale is quiet,
charming and unobtrusive now, but was once an important
market town. Most dales are named after their river, so you
might expect this one to be named Uredale or Yoredale. That did
not sound right, but Wensleydale did. Edward I granted Wensley
a charter in 1306, but in 1563 it was devastated by the plague
and it never recovered. Its market and trade went to Leyburn,
then a hamlet in the parish of Wensley. Later Charles II granted
Leyburn a market charter.*

*This walk is full of interest for all the family. It starts from a
lively spacious town, continues high along a limestone scarp,
passes remnants of Wensleydale's largest lead mine, visits one
of the most impressive churches in the dale, and returns over
quiet pastures ideal for bird watching.*

Start: The Town Hall (now a multi-store) in the market place,
Leyburn (GR112905)

Total distance: 9km (5½ miles)

Height gain: 60m (197 feet)

Difficulty: Easy walking on good clear tracks and paths

1 From the Town Hall, walk towards the top of the market place
(west). Cross the main road and continue on to the right of the
Dalesman's Club, following several signs directing you to 'The
Shawl'. At the street end, turn left and, a few steps along, go
through a gate on your right. Walk on over the fine grassy turf
and continue over several stiled pastures. Ignore a footpath
that descends left. The route is never in any doubt. Enjoy the
view over the lovely, now wide dale of Wensley, with the
magnificent Penhill dominating all.

*This natural terrace, 250m above sea level and extending
for two miles, is known as Leyburn Shawl. The name shawl
perhaps originates from the Anglo-Saxon 'schale', meaning
easily splitting rock. Local legend says it is named after the
shawl of Mary Queen of Scots, which she dropped as she
fled along the escarpment from Bolton Castle (walk 6)
where she was imprisoned. The Victorians had tea festivals
on the 'shawl'; in 1845 more than a thousand people had*

tea in a grand marquee and more than two thousand joined in the dancing afterwards.

2 Continue on to pass through a gate into glorious woodland, with a fine stone wall to your right and deciduous tree-clad slopes dropping steeply left to the vale. Here, where the path comes close to the edge of the slope, young children should be reminded to take care.

3 As the slope becomes less steep, ignore a wide grassy track which drops left and carry on along the pleasing high level way, with Addlebrough (Walk 5) coming into view. Continue on the rim of the scarp just inside Warren Wood and, on reaching a wire fence on the edge of trees, and just before a new planting of trees, climb a stile into a more open area, with several huge beeches. Follow the path, half-left, to take another stile into a pasture.

4 Keep on the same general diagonal and gently descend to a stile beside a gate. Stride on to pass, over a wire fence on the left, scattered boulders and depressions in the ground, believed to be part of an ancient settlement and field system. Join a farm track and continue on it to pass through a gate. Walk on the track to a junction of tracks, where you bear right to pass Tullis Cote farmhouse, on your left.

5 Just before you wind left, round the last outbuildings of the farm, pause and look ahead to see the arched stone barn. This was once a peat store for Keld Head Mine, over which you have been walking. Go on left, with the beck over the wall on your right. Where the track swings left, go ahead down another narrower track to pass a huge chimney and then the engine shed of the old mine. Once it employed three hundred men,

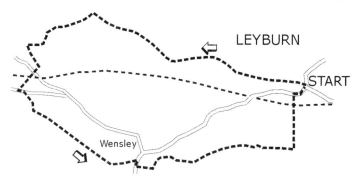

who earned 12½ pence a day. The mine extended for a mile into the hill and needed a two-mile long flue, which ran along the ground. The mine was closed in 1888 because of severe flooding and the low price of lead.

6 Follow the continuing lane as it winds left and then right, passing various old buildings, all very interesting, belonging to the mine. Stroll on to a narrow road, which you cross. Pass through a signposted stile and continue ahead to the railway track. Cross and walk on to a gate in the right corner to join a narrow road. Walk left for 100m to take a well made track into woodland on your right. A short way along, turn left as directed by the signpost, through larch, to a gate out of the trees. Bear right and walk a farm track. Immediately before a cattle grid, climb the arrowed slope left and wind round right on a very pleasing track.

7 At the corner of the fence, on your left, follow the arrow directing you diagonally across glorious parkland. Climb the stile over the fence, just before an enormous oak and continue on the same diagonal to a gate onto the reinforced access track to Bolton Hall. Stroll left into the village of Wensley.

8 Pass the sloping, triangular, tiny, village green on your left, with its pump and a seat just made for a picnic. While in this lovely village visit its glorious church, just below the green on the Middleham road. Then walk on along this road to cross a bridge over a stream and turn left beyond. Climb the peaceful lane and follow it as it winds right, to take a waymarked gate on the right. Continue ahead and walk the stiled way until you are directed left, uphill, along the edge of a small wood to a stile at the top corner of the trees. Beyond, walk on to a stile, on your right, just beyond the next corner of the wood. Cross a small footbridge and head on to the next stile.

9 Continue ahead over many small stiled pastures. When you near a barn note the several red painted arrows directing you over a stile to a footpath that keeps you left of the building, but still keeping ahead. Then drop down to a gully-like path, Low Wood Lane. Walk left. The way soon improves and climbs steadily to the A-road into Leybyrn. A very short walk returns to the market square.

Along the Way

Holy Trinity Church, Wensley was built in 1245 on the site of an ancient Saxon church is one of the most impressive in the dales. Parts of the church were added in the 14th and 15th century and the tower in the 18th.

Glorious carved oak stalls in the chancel have poppy heads and carvings of heraldic beasts. On the floor of the sanctuary is a splendid brass which commemorate Sir Simon Wenslawe, a 14th-century priest. The church has a wonderful carved screen and an ancient wooden reliquary from Easby Abbey, which is thought to have contained the remains of St Agatha. There are 17th-century curtained box pews installed by the third Duke of Bolton. Look for the Jacobean font (1662) and for the standard of the Dales Volunteers raised by Lord Bolton during the Napoleanic Wars. The church has many more treasures which youngsters will enjoy finding, and time should be allowed for this on the walk.

Lead mining

Lead mining once was an important industry, especially on the hills above this walk. In the Middle Ages, the abbeys obtained the right to mine the lead. It became such a valuable commodity that it was worth using high cost teams of pack-horses to carry it away. Smelting lead produced toxic fumes and tall chimneys, such as you pass on this walk, were needed to carry them away. Long flues were also built, just above ground level (you have walked over one on the walk. Inside both, soot containing valuable lead, condensed on the walls and youngsters were sent up or along to scrape it down or out.

9
Middleham to Coverham Church

*From either end of Wensleydale, Middleham is reached by a hill.
It is a wonderful place to start a walk and time should be
allowed for exploring. Visit the castle; look for two squares, both
with a market cross; find the memorial to Queen Victoria and
read the plaques commemorating highlights of her life; find the
old school with a tower; wander over the cobbled alleys; and go
to the church dedicated to a Saxon saint who was strangled by
two Danish women. Middleham was once the home of a king.
Today, this lovely small town is renowned in the racing world for
the breeding and training of horses.*

Start: The lower cobbled square at Middleham (GR128878)

Total distance: 10.5km (6½ miles)

Height gain: 170m (560 feet)

Difficulty: Generally easy walk

1 From the square go uphill for a very short distance and turn
left up the first narrow, cobbled way, lined with pretty cottages.
Go ahead along the signposted lane, with the castle to your
right. Just before a gate across the lane, take a waymarked
gated stile, on the right, and head diagonally left to a gate in
the fence. Stride over the next pasture towards a rounded
hillock. This is William's Hill, Ring and Bailey, the site of a
Norman motte and bailey castle, which was probably occupied
for many years. Children will like to climb up the outer
fortification and explore the moat. From here you have a fine
view of Middleham Castle, which replaced the one you are
standing on.

2 Retrace your steps to the lane and turn right to go through
the gate across it. At the signpost take the path, sweeping
diagonally left, across the large rolling pasture, following the
signpost directions for 'Stepping Stones'. Continue on the
same diagonal across three more stiled pastures to come to
a wall. Descend the short slope to the side of the delightful
River Cover and the fine solid stepping stone across it. This is
a lovely corner, where if the river is not in spate, children will
want to paddle and cross the stones.

35

3 Then walk, right, along the riverbank, with the hurrying water to your left and beyond, Witton Banks rearing upwards. Continue on the often muddy path, through woodland, to enter an idyllic pasture, surrounded by slopes, where you will all want to linger. Leave this delectable spot by a gate in the far top corner to climb steps, taking you high above the river. Follow the well-waymarked path (muddy) up and down little steps, keeping you well above the eroded riverbank. Finally you descend into open pasture beside the river on your left. Ignore path climbing up the slope and wind round the edge of a waymarked wall, beside the river, and then climb right. Ascend the steepish slope and pause at the first flattish area to look back on dramatic Cover Scar. Then go on up to a post with lots of waymarks. Here turn left to continue, right, alongside Cover Banks, a narrow wood on your left.

4 Near the end of the trees, take a stile into the pines and in a couple of steps take another out of the copse. Then descend a clear path as it drops steadily towards the riverbank. Go on down a track, marked by a white-topped post, beneath beech and ash to cross the delightful River Cover on the sturdy Hullo Bridge.

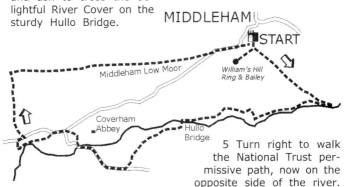

5 Turn right to walk the National Trust permissive path, now on the opposite side of the river. Continue on, with a fence to your right, until you reach a wall and a waymark directing you up the pasture. At the top, wind right before the wall and then take the stile, on the left, to join Hanghow Lane by a stile.

6 Go right along the lane to cross the high-arched bridge over the lovely Cover river, still dancing over its rocky bed. Just beyond, turn right along a track, to pass a dwelling on the left, once a mill built by the monks of Coverham Abbey. Take a gate on the left just beyond the former mill-race and climb up

beside the tempestuous flow to a gate and on to visit the 13th century church of the Holy Trinity.

7 Leave the churchyard by the lychgate. Ignore the immediate left turn and walk left for a short way along Coverham Lane to take the signposted footpath on the left. Cross a small stream by a gated bridge. Climb the stile just ahead and bear right. Continue on the path, which leads into a wide track with the River Cover far below on the left. Go through a gate and carry on across a pasture to a gate onto an access track. Turn right and walk on to pass through large gates – youngsters will enjoy the carvings on top of the posts. At the road bear right for a few metres and then cross and start your gentle climb up the bridleway, signposted by a board, which says 'The Forbidden Corner';- the bridleway post is almost obscured by the board.

8 Climb the metalled way and where it divides, take the right branch and go on a pleasing track as it passes the ornate gardens on the right, of Fern Gill House, with deciduous woodland to the left. Go through more large gates and walk right along a reinforced bridleway.

9 Very soon the way moves left, unmarked and away from the wall on the right, to cross Middleham Low Moor, which you might find yourselves sharing with the horses from Middleham. Keep on the same general direction across the moor to reach the road into Middleham by the town's name board. Cross here and go through a gated stile in the wall. Walk across two stiled pastures and then go through the stile onto the lane taken at the outset of the walk. Turn left to return to the Middleham, having perhaps left time for exploring the delightful small town.

Along the Way

Holy Trinity was in use until the 1970s, and was the church for all who lived in Coverdale. Today the dale has few buildings and the church is maintained by the Churches Conservation Trust. In the Middle Ages lead and coal mines contributed to the prosperity of the neighbourhood and quarries were worked for stone, used for millstones. Then the church would have been full of parishioners from its extensive parish. Holy Trinity lies close to Coverham Abbey, which was typical of most monasteries in having a parish church at its gate. (There is no access now from the church to Coverham Abbey.)

37

10
Jervaulx Abbey

Below Leyburn, Wensleydale opens out and the River Ure dons a more matronly pose after its earlier petulance. From Witton Fell you look down on a delightful pastoral scene of magnificent trees, large scattered farms, winding rivers and extensive parkland. From East Witton the road through the dale continues to the abbey of Jervaulx Norman -French for Uredale. Here in 1156 a Cistercian monastery was founded after the monks spent eleven years at Fors, near Askrigg, unable to survive attacks of unfriendly locals, the wolves and several years of bad weather (see walk 4). All the family will enjoy this walk through this delightful end of Wensleydale.

Start: The car park opposite the entrance to the abbey (GR169856)

Total distance: 12km (7½ miles)

Height gain: Virtually none

Difficulty: None; wonderfully easy. This is a most straightforward walk and one that youngsters could map read for the family

1 Cross the road from the car park and go through a gate to walk on to visit the ruined abbey. As you enter there is a donation box for the abbey's upkeep and where you pay for an information leaflet. Wander through the picturesque ruins and when you have had your fill, pick up the wide track that continues through the fine parkland, with the abbey to your left and a delightful house to your right. Follow the way as it winds through tree-topped small hillocks. Pass some little pools and then, at the end of the track, go past the lodge and turn left onto Kilgram Lane.

2 Stroll the quiet lane until you can cross Kilgram Bridge, sturdily strengthened with stone arches underneath against a River Ure in spate. Just beyond, on the right, is a rather neglected walkway with flood holes below, put there for times when the now wide and surging river flooded its banks. A short way beyond the bridge, take the footpath on the left. Walk the stiled way, watching out for a glimpse of the Jervaulx Abbey through the trees on the left. Beyond a gate the waymarked path turns sharp right and heads up towards Woodhouse farm.

Follow the waymarks carefully as these lead you to the left of farm and then left again in front of a dutch barn.

3 Carry on ahead over the well waymarked stiled way, which brings you to the edge of Thornton Steward. Walk on along a narrow track, which soon winds right and comes to the small

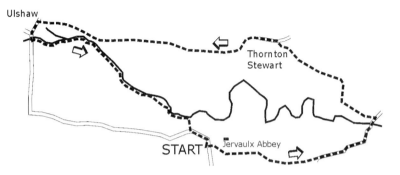

green in the centre of the village. Here there is a seat under a large tree and just the place for a stop. Behind the green is an unusual castellated house built in the early 19th century by Captain Horn, the village eccentric.

4 Stroll on (west) through the village to the end of the road at Manor House farm. Go through the gates and stride on the metalled way as it gently descends with mixed deciduous woodland to your right and with willow and Scots pine woodland to the left. The willow flushes bright orange in the early spring contrasting strikingly with the dark green of the pines. And then you come to St Oswald's Church in its lovely isolated position, which you will want to visit.

5 Leave the churchyard by the opposite corner from the one you entered and walk on along the wide greensward way. Keep ahead passing through the pastures, by several small green gates. At a green farm gate, go on ahead to pass, on your right, splendid Danby Hall. A few steps on join a wide access track and follow it as it winds left before continuing ahead. Go through a gate, leaving the fine parkland behind to walk on past Danby Low Mill, which overlooks the River Ure. Continue on the track until you can join a quiet road, with Ulshaw Church ahead. At the T-junction turn left to cross the beautiful Ulshaw bridge over a very wide River Ure.

Nearby East Witton was another village stricken by the plague. In 1563 its market was ordered to be removed to Ulshaw Bridge and East Witton never again recovered its prominence.

6 Walk on to the triangle of grass in front of Cover Bridge Inn. Wind left to cross Cover Bridge and at its end turn left onto the footpath that runs beside the River Cover. As you stroll the raised path watch for kingfishers and dippers. Watch also for where the Cover flows into the Ure, not easy to spot because of several small islands and then go on to pass the mill once more, now being splendidly refurbished. Continue on past a large reed-fringed pond, home to swans, coots and moorhens.

In 1999 clutches of eggs were laid and hatched successfully but sadly and puzzlingly – few chicks survived. In September of that year, the culprits for the depredation were discovered: 102 eels and a 6.4kg (14lb) pike were netted and taken to another pond.

7 Keep on along the lovely riverside way until your path is barred by a fence. Go through a gate on the right and walk beside glorious beeches on the left, to join the road. Turn left and stroll on. Wind round, right, with the road, and the car park and a small restaurant, lie on the opposite side of the road.

Along the Way

Four hundred years after it was established at Jervaulx, the abbey was dissolved and its abbot hanged at Tyburn. Today, the ruins are in private hands and you can wander at will below the ornate arches, dawdle round the remnants of cloisters and sit on the stone seats in the chapter house where the monks once sat. It is a beautiful corner; in summer vibrant purple aubrietia hangs from the stones of the abbey, rolling parkland stretches away from the old stones and in summer wildflowers cover the sward.

John Wayn‹

The True Crime Story of the Killer Clown

Table of Contents

Introduction

The world is home to over seven billion people. In it, there have been great human beings: genius scientists that found cures or solutions to humanity's biggest problems; brilliant engineers that have created technology that has advanced us, giving us the ability to carry an almost infinite amount of information in a handheld device and taking us to space; and noble leaders who have fought the powers of tyrants and succeeded, liberating their people and winning back their rights.

But, as in any great community in existence, in the same way that our planet can harbor greatness, it can also create evil.

Such is the case of **John Wayne Gacy**, a man shrouded in darkness. After a troubled childhood and low self-esteem due to his small height and obesity, he attempted to live a normal life but couldn't control his sadistic urges.

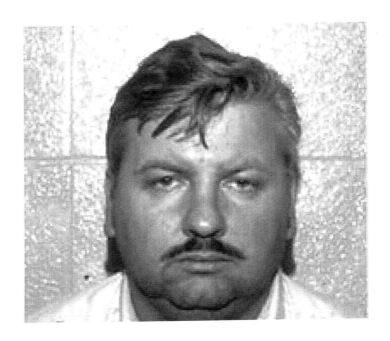

Despite his attempts at marriage and family, living as a well-known member of his community and being involved in politics, his urges to dominate, torture and murder young men led him to become a monster of the worst kind: mixing sexual fantasies with terrible actions. It shocked the entire country when his true identity was revealed.

In the following book, we will tell the story of the **Killer Clown**, the identity that John Wayne Gacy adopted to win over the people who knew him, especially his victims. An identity that ended up taking the man over, and who in his mind drove him to kill, along with the other personalities he possessed.

Prepare yourself; the gruesome actions of John Wayne Gacy are not for the lighthearted.

One last thing: thanks for downloading this book!

Part 1

Beginnings of a Monster

Every story has a beginning. Every human being, great or evil, was once just a harmless, small child. John Wayne Gacy was no different.

He was born on March 17, 1942, in Chicago, Illinois, the only son and second of three children to John Stanley Gacy, an auto repair mechanist and World War I veteran; and Marion Elaine Robinson, a homemaker. Gacy's paternal grandparents had immigrated to the United States from Poland, and he also had Danish heritage.

As a boy, Gacy soon became overweight, a trait that would lead to a serious lack of self-esteem as he grew up. But it wasn't his body that made his childhood a traumatizing period of his life. Despite his positive relationship with his sisters and mother, his father was an abusive alcoholic. One of his pastimes after arriving home from a tough day at work was to go down to the basement and drink brandy until he was drunk. Meanwhile, his terrified wife and children would wait for him at the dinner table until he finally finished and decided to eat. Failure to comply with this tradition meant taking a beating from the violent man.

Gacy often sought approval from his father, but never received a hint of paternal pride at all. Instead, the man would heap physical and verbal abuse on him from as early as age four, when he was beaten with a leather belt for disarranging some work components his father had assembled. Gacy was often belittled and compared with his sisters by his father, who labeled him "dumb and stupid," and made him feel, in every single way, that he was not good enough for the man. Despite all of this, Gacy stated till his last days that he had never hated his dad.

His father would often whip the children with a razor strap until he felt satisfied that they were punished. Such was the case when, in 1949, he was informed that his son and another boy had sexually fondled a young girl. Gacy began to fear his father's punishments so much, that later that year, he hid the fact that was being molested by a family friend--a man who would take him on truck rides and fondle him. Gacy believed his father would blame him for the abuse like he did everything else. However, his sister Karen stated many years after that the abuse had made them all stronger, having to toughen up against the beatings. She also added that the fact that Gacy did not cry while receiving the beatings made their father angrier as time passed.

Gacy was kept out of school sports activities due to a congenital heart condition, which, added to his already clumsy overweight body, caused him to be a victim of mockery and bullying. He was alienated by his peers and his self-esteem suffered as a result. At the age of 11, Gacy was struck on the forehead by a swing. The trauma caused a blood clot in his brain that went unnoticed until he reached the age of 16, when it was finally treated. However, before its discovery, Gacy would often suffer blackouts severe enough for him to spend months in the hospital, and consequently suffered in his grades. His father, a true bastard, believed that the blackouts were an attempt to gain sympathy and attention, and went so far as to say he was faking it while his son lay on a hospital bed.

Even one of Gacy's few friends, a boy named Richard Dalke, was present during several instances when Gacy's father abused him. He recalled instances when his father ridiculed or beat Gacy without reason. He once described an occasion when the man began shouting at his son with no provocation, then began to beat him. Gacy would simply protect himself by lifting his hands, never once striking back at his abuser.

John Wayne Gacy began an important incursion into politics at the age of 18, seeking the acceptance he had never received from his dad. He worked as an assistant precinct captain for a Democratic Party candidate, and despite further criticism from his father, became a candidate himself that same year. His father bought him a car, keeping the title in his own name until it was paid in full, but Gacy was only allowed to use it if he did as he was told. He grew tired of his father's constant controlling and drove to Las Vegas, Nevada, leaving his home.

There, he briefly worked for an ambulance service before being transferred to work as a mortuary attendant. It was around this age that he began to realize his attraction to men, experiencing great turmoil over his sexuality. One night, he was left alone in the embalming room, and admittedly clambered into the coffin of a deceased male teenager, embracing and touching the body before feeling great shock at his own actions. This experience led him to return to Chicago, only three months after having left.

Gacy was allowed to return home, driving back the same day after he experimented sexually with the corpse. He enrolled at Northwestern Business College, despite having failed to graduate from high school. He managed to graduate from the college, one of his few achievements during his early years, and got a job at the Nunn-Bush Shoe Company. He was transferred to Springfield, Illinois in 1964 by the same company, and there he met his first wife: Marlynn Myers, a co-worker. They married in September of the same year.

Marlynn was the daughter of a businessman who purchased three Kentucky Fried Chicken (yes, the same Kentucky Fried Chicken we all know) restaurants in Iowa, and soon offered Gacy the opportunity to manage them. Around this year, Gacy joined the Jaycees (US Junior Chamber) and climbed the ranks. When he and Marlynn moved to Waterloo, Iowa so Gacy could manage the fast food restaurants, he continued to work with the Jaycees, even being named "Outstanding Vice-President" of the Waterloo Jaycees in 1967. However, there was a darker side to the Jaycee organization in Waterloo, which involved prostitution, pornography, and drugs. Gacy was intimately involved in this side, and further explored his homosexuality, cheating on his wife regularly. She gave birth to two children: a son in 1967 and a daughter in 1968. Gacy felt happy for the first time in his life. His father even approached him at some point in 1967 after the birth of his grandson, and apologized for the physical and mental abuse he had inflicted upon his son, informing him: "Son, I was wrong about you."

Gacy continued his Jaycee activities and drugs become involved. He even opened a club in his basement, where he would invite employees to drink alcohol and play pool. Suspiciously, only young males were invited, and many of them became Gacy's sexual partners.

This secret life became more and more a part of Gacy's identity, and in August 1967, he committed his first criminal act. A 15-year-old named Donald Voorhees, son of a fellow Jaycee, was lured by Gacy to his house, under the promise of some pornographic movies. Gacy supplied Voorhees with copious amounts of alcohol, and then persuaded the teenager to perform oral sex on him. Other youths were sexually abused in a similar manner, including one who Gacy encouraged to have sex with his wife before blackmailing him into performing oral sex on him.

It all came crashing down on Gacy in March 1968, when Donald Voorhees told his father what Gacy had done. Voorhees Sr. did not hesitate for a minute, informing the police and having Gacy arrested and charged with oral sodomy on Voorhees, and the attempted assault of a 16-year-old. He denied his actions, adopting a victim's position and demanded to take a polygraph test. It didn't go well for him, the results indicating suspicious nervous activity while denying any wrongdoing in relation to both teenagers' accusations. Gacy continued to deny any wrongdoing, stating the accusations were politically motivated. Despite receiving support from his Jaycee companions, he was indicted on May 10, 1968, authorities considering him guilty.

Gacy was desperate to protect his image, and facing the inevitable trial, decided to take drastic measures to stay out of prison. On August 30, 1968, he persuaded an 18-year-old employee named Russell Schroeder to physically assault Voorhees to discourage the boy from testifying against him. They agreed on a $300 payment, and the plan was for the youth to lure Voorhees to a secluded spot, spray *Mace* in his face and beat the young man up. The plan went excellently, everything going as Gacy had decided... that is, until Voorhees reported the assault to the police, identifying his attacker. Schroeder was arrested the next day, and despite initially denying involvement, caved in to the interrogation, and confessed that he had acted on Gacy's behest. Gacy was arrested and additionally charged with hiring Schroeder to assault Voorhees. He also received psychiatric evaluations over a period of 17 days, and it was concluded that Gacy suffered from antisocial personality disorder (ASPD), and that he was mentally competent to stand trial.

He stood trial, and despite insisting that Voorhees had offered him sexual services and not the other way around, he was not believed, and convicted of sodomy on December 3, 1968, and sentenced to 10 years at

Anamosa State Penitentiary. That same day, his wife Marlynn filed for divorce. She requested possession of the home, property, and alimony payments. The divorce was finalized on September 18, 1969, and Gacy never saw her nor their children ever again.

Inside prison, he quickly gained a model reputation, and worked hard to get along with his fellow inmates. After becoming head cook, he joined the inmate Jaycees and recruited additional members. Using his political abilities, he negotiated an inmates' pay increase for their work in the mess hall and supervised projects that improved living conditions for the inmates, such as the installation of a golf course.

He applied for parole in June 1969, but was denied. He began to study school courses and obtained a diploma. When he received the news of his father's death from cirrhosis two days after Christmas Day, 1969, he collapsed on the floor, sobbing uncontrollably. A request for compassionate leave to attend his dad's funeral was denied.

His desire for freedom would pay off however, when he was granted parole with 12 months' probation in June 1970, having served just 18 months of his 10-year sentence. He would have to relocate to Chicago to live with his mother as one of the conditions of his probation, the other being that he had to respect a 10 p.m. curfew.

Gacy stated to a friend that he would "never go back to jail," and he relocated to Chicago within the 24 hours after his release on June 19. Despite getting a job as a cook in a restaurant, Gacy had not changed his ways. On February 12, 1971, he was charged with sexually assaulting a teenager. The boy claimed he had been lured into Gacy's car and taken to the man's home, where he had attempted to rape the young man. This sticky situation resolved itself positively for Gacy, when the boy failed to appear in court and the Iowa Board of Parole did not hear about it--an event that would have violated the conditions they had set. In October 1971, Gacy's parole was finalized.

He received financial help from his mother, and bought a house in an area of Cook County. The home, 8213 West Summerdale Avenue, would become the resting place of many young men, specifically the four-foot deep crawl space in the basement. In August 1971, he and his mother moved into the house, and Gacy became engaged to a divorcee with two daughters named Carole Hoff. Hoff had been a high school girlfriend of his, and a friend of his younger sister. She moved in with him, and his mother moved out shortly after the wedding on July 1, 1972. Around this time, he was arrested again and charged with battery after another young man reported to the police that Gacy had flashed a fake sheriff's badge at him, and after luring him into his car, forced him to perform oral sex. The charges were dropped because the boy attempted to blackmail Gacy. Despite the initial jail time that Gacy suffered, he would become luckier and luckier as time passed when it came to paying for his crimes.

Gacy started a business of his own in 1972, a company he named "PDM Contractors", the initials standing for "Painting, Decorating, and Maintenance." He offered minor repair work services, but expanded to interior design, remodeling and landscaping, among other things. This company would be one of his best "tools" for capturing young boys.

Such was the case in 1973, when Gacy traveled to Florida to view property he had purchased. He took a young male employee with him, and on the first night in the hotel room, raped him. The young man slept on a beach for the remainder of the trip. When they returned to Chicago, the youth drove to Gacy's home and beat him until Gacy's mother-in-law intervened. Once the employee was gone, she asked Gacy what had happened, and he stated that the youth had been angry over not being paid for poor quality work.

Gacy's façade was perfect; his neighbors were quickly "falling in love" with him. He was considered a happy, helpful man, who would host annual summer parties. He became more active in the Democratic Party, offering PDM employee services free of charge. He was rewarded for his community services and earned the title of precinct captain. During one of his activities as director of Chicago's annual Polish Constitution Day Parade, Gacy met and was photographed with the then First Lady, Rosalynn Carter, on May 6, 1978. The famous photograph even has her autograph, an embarrassing reminder to the Secret Service – who gave special clearance to Gacy – that they still had a bit to learn, once they found out who and what John Wayne Gacy truly was.

It was around this time of his life that Gacy adopted his newest identity. In 1975, Gacy joined a local Moose Club. He found out about a "Jolly Joker" clown club, where men and women would dress as clowns and participate in fundraising events and parades, as well as volunteer to cheer up kids in the hospital. That same year, he began to be known as "Pogo the Clown." He created his own outfit and makeups, contrasting the typical rounded features with sharp corners, making him look more menacing than the usual clown. He performed at local parties and charitable events, gaining even more of a reputation as a friendly, funny man. He would even take his clown suit with him to drink at a local bar.

While this might have been seen as a harmless and funny thing to do for those around him, the truth was much darker: a part of Gacy was beginning to "become" Pogo the Clown, his broken psyche adopted it as a personality within his mind, a being with desires--evil desires.

We have told you what you need to know about how Gacy's life began and developed. For all that we have talked about rape and sodomy, forced blowjobs and intimidation, the story is still to take a turn for the worse...

Part 2

Evil Unleashed

Despite his past actions, his former crimes and darkness, Gacy was a man loved by many. His neighbors, friends, and fellow members of associations and political parties looked up to him and respected him. They saw his criminal record as mistakes made by a good man. To them, he was a caring, generous, and pleasant man who cared about society. None of those who loved him would have imagined the killer he would become, shortly after New Year's Day in 1972, when Gacy committed the first of many gruesome murders. Let us begin, then...

The first death was the most curious, yet every murderer has to begin somewhere. On January 2, 1972, Gacy picked up a 16-year-old named Timothy Jack McCoy from Chicago's Greyhound bus terminal, taking him on a sightseeing tour of the city. The two then went back to Gacy's home, where he told the lad that he would take him back to the station in time to catch his bus. The next morning, McCoy would become his first victim. The murder happened under strange circumstances. According to Gacy, he woke to see McCoy standing in the doorway with a knife in his hand. Alarmed, he rose from his bed, and McCoy raised his arms in fear, cutting

Gacy in the process. Gacy took the knife from his grip, banged him against a wall, and kicked him. The boy tried to defend himself, but Gacy closed in for the kill, stabbing him in the chest repeatedly as he wrestled for his life. He went to the kitchen moments later and found that the young man had been preparing breakfast, hence the kitchen knife. Out of fear of discovery, Gacy buried McCoy in his aforementioned crawl space, later covering the grave with concrete. Gacy admitted years later that despite emotionally not enjoying the kill, he'd had an orgasm as he took McCoy's life, and realized that death was the ultimate thrill.

Two years later, in January 1974, Gacy killed again, this time without excuse. The victim was between 14 and 18 years old, a boy that Gacy had lured to his home. He strangled him, and then buried him in the crawl space.

It was in 1975 when Gacy realized sexual advances on his employees were not the only things he could do to them. At that point, his sexual adventures increased, having recently admitted to his wife Carole that he was bisexual and promising her they would never again have sex. She began to find gay pornography inside the house and frequently saw Gacy with teenage boys around the home. In July of the same year, Gacy arrived at the home of one such employee, a 15-year-old named Anthony Antonucci, who was resting after having injured his foot at work. Gacy gave him alcohol, then wrestled the boy to the floor when he was distracted, and cuffed his hands behind his back. Antonucci watched Gacy leave the room and freed himself; one of his wrists had been badly cuffed and was left loose. As Gacy returned, Antonucci leapt onto him. Being a member of the school wrestling team decided the fight, as Antonucci tore the keys from Gacy's possession and cuffed Gacy's hand behind his back. Stupidly, Antonucci uncuffed Gacy in exchange for him leaving the house. Gacy escaped, humiliated but safe. Antonucci later stated that Gacy had admitted as he lay cuffed: "Not only are you the only one who got out of the cuffs; you got them on me."

Barely one week later, on July 29, 1975, a 17-year-old employee called John Butkovitch disappeared. He had threatened Gacy over unpaid work the day before, something that a few people were aware of. The truth is, Butkovitch became another of Gacy's victims. Gacy lured him to his home while his wife and stepdaughter were traveling, stating that he wanted to settle the issue of wages. Once inside the home, Gacy somehow conned him into putting the cuffs on, before strangling him to death and burying him under the concrete floor of his garage. The young man's car was found abandoned with his wallet inside, the keys still in the ignition. His parents suspected Gacy, and he received a call from the boy's father, leading him to reply that he would be happy to help search for the boy. Gacy was questioned about the disappearance by the police, and admitted that the youth had gone to his home with two friends, but the three had left after reaching an agreement. Butkovitch's parents never believed Gacy, and urged police to investigate him further for years.

A few months later, in October, Gacy's marriage reached the boiling point and Carole filed for divorce, claiming Gacy was unfaithful with other women, respectfully keeping his homosexuality a secret. They continued to live together at 8213 West Summerdale until February of 1976, when she moved out with her daughters. Gacy's façade held after this event, but he began to show signs of his dark behavior more often now that he lived alone. Neighbors saw him entering and leaving his home at early hours of the morning, lights turning on and off at late hours, and young males in or around the house. One neighbor recalled that she and her son had often heard muffled screaming, shouting, and crying coming from a nearby home, understanding eventually to her horror (after Gacy's arrest) what the sounds had represented.

One month after the divorce was finalized, Gacy went on another "cruise," the term he used for his excursions to have sex with young males, excursions that would promptly end in death. He abducted and murdered Darrell Sampson, an 18-year-old. Sampson was last seen alive on April 6, 1976. Just five weeks later, May 14th, a 15-year-old named Randall Reffett went missing while walking home from high school. He was gagged with a cloth and died of asphyxiation. At a difference of mere hours, a 14-year-old named Samuel Stapleton disappeared in similar circumstances as he walked home. Both corpses were buried in the same grave in Gacy's crawl space.

On June 3, 1976, a 17-year-old named Michael Bonnin was strangled by Gacy, using a ligature method. Gacy buried the corpse in the crawl space. Ten days later, Gacy murdered a 16-year-old named William Carroll, who ended up buried directly beneath Gacy's kitchen. Four other males were buried in this common grave. Two were identified; they were teenagers aged 16 and 17 years old. The other two were a man in his mid or late twenties and a boy between 15 and 19 years old, who was only identified as having dark hair, and died by strangling.

On August 21, an 18-year-old named David Cram, who had been employed by Gacy just one month before, moved into his house. The next day, Gacy got him drunk and conned him into putting handcuffs on. The first thing he did, once the cuffs were on, was to tell Cram he was going to rape him. Unfortunately for Gacy, Cram was ex-Army, and kicked him in the face. He freed himself from the handcuffs as Gacy lay on the floor. For inexplicable reasons, Cram continued to live at Gacy's home for another month, until Gacy showed up at his bedroom door and told him that it was better if he just "gave him what he wanted." Cram saw something dark in Gacy at that moment (finally) and left the home, also leaving PDM Contractors, though he periodically worked for Gacy for the following two years. Not long after Cram moved out, another employee named Michael Rossi, 18, moved into the house.

Gacy killed again between August and October 1976. The bodies were placed above the corpses that had been buried in a common grave. One was a male between 21 and 27 years old, the other a younger male between 17 and 21. A PDM employee recalled digging a trench in the area where the victim was buried, around October of the same year. A few weeks later, on October 24, 1976, Gacy abducted two teenage friends named Kenneth Parker and Michael Marino. They were last seen outside a restaurant. Gacy strangled them at his home, and buried them in the same grave in the crawl space. Just two days later, an employee of PDM Contractors, named William Bundy, 19, disappeared. He was also strangled and found buried in the crawl space beneath Gacy's master bedroom.

Another employee disappeared in December 1976: 17-year-old Gregory Godzik, last seen by his girlfriend after driving her home following a date. He had only been working at PDM for a few weeks at the time of his disappearance, and had also helped Gacy build some kind of trench in his crawl space. His car was later found abandoned. Godzik's family contacted Gacy, asking if he had any information on the disappearance. Gacy informed them that the young man had decided to run away from home, telling Gacy before he did so. He also claimed to have received a recorded answering machine message a few days after Godzik had gone missing, but told the family he had deleted it. In truth, Godzik had been murdered, just like so many others.

A month later, on January 20, 1977, Gacy killed 19-year-old John Szyc, a young man who had known both Butkovich and Godzik. Gacy lured him to his house by pretending he was interested in buying his Plymouth

Satellite, which would be significant later. He was strangled and buried in Gacy's crawl space like the rest, but Gacy kept his ring and portable TV, and sold Szyc's car to an employee named Michael Rossi.

By now, Gacy had killed and buried quite a few young men beneath his home. More than a dozen bodies lay in the basement beneath his house, and of course, they began to decompose. This process of rot caused the house to exhibit a terrible odor that Gacy could not remove or cover by any means. The layers of concrete he laid on top of the graves did nothing to stop the smell. When Carole was still living there, he would often evasively state that he would talk to the public plumbing services, blaming the smell on the water that typically flooded the crawl space. Carole herself believed there was a nest with dead rats beneath them. On two separate occasions, there were parties at the home: a cowboy party, then a Hawaiian themed one in the backyard. Despite having a pleasant time, some guests remarked later that the event had been slightly marred by the foul odor coming from the basement of Gacy's home. Luckily for him, none of the people involved recognized the smell for what it had truly been: the smell of rotting human corpses.

Gacy murdered another unidentified young man of around 25 years of age, between December 1976 and March 1977. His body was buried beneath Jon

Prestidge, who had been visiting Chicago on March 15 when he was killed by Gacy. Gacy killed another youth shortly after, though not many details were known about timing or identity. He was aged between 17 and 21.

In March 1977, Gacy became a construction supervisor for a company named PE Systems, a firm that specialized in remodeling drugstores. Through this job, Gacy regularly traveled around the country, and had more access to drugs for personal use, for recreation, and for other, darker, measures. He became engaged to a woman he had been dating in April 1977, and she moved into the house. However, only two months later, they called the engagement off and she left the home. Gacy killed just a month later, a 19-year-old named Matthew Bowman, who was buried with tourniquet Gacy had used to strangle him still gripping the boy's neck.

It was in August 1977 when the car Gacy sold came back to haunt him. Michael Rossi, the youth who had bought Szyc's car from Gacy, was arrested for stealing gasoline while driving the car. The arresting officer looked up the license plate number and it took the police to Gacy's house, since Rossi had been living with him at the time. Gacy, being an expert at lying, quickly maneuvered out of the sticky situation by telling the officers who arrived at his home that Szyc had sold him the car so he could leave town with the money. The police accepted this explanation without further investigation.

Gacy began pursuing his ex-wife Carole Hoff again in late 1977, hoping to win her back. The plan failed, and she got engaged to another man the next year. Gacy killed six more young men before the end of that year, all of them between 16 and 21 years old. The first was an 18 year old, Robert Gilroy, son of a Chicago police sergeant, who Gacy suffocated and buried in the crawl space. There are theories that the boy was killed or at least held captive by an accomplice, since the exact same date when the young man disappeared coincided with one of Gacy's work travels to another state. Further mysterious events would continue to reinforce the theory that Gacy wasn't working alone in all of his murders. Ten days after Gilroy was abducted, a 19-year-old U.S Marine called John Mowery went missing while walking back home from his mother's. Mowery was also strangled and buried in the crawl space.

On October 17, Gacy murdered a 21-year-old from Minnesota, Russell Nelson. He was suffocated and subsequently buried in the crawl space. The next month, Gacy took the lives of two young men: 16-year-old Robert Winch and 20-year-old Tommy Boling, a young man who was father to a recently born baby. Both were strangled to death and buried in the crawl space beneath the hallway. Still, Gacy's secret was safe, despite living above a graveyard he had created.

Three weeks later, another U.S. Marine disappeared, a 19-year-old called David Talsma, who had been on the way to attend a rock concert when he disappeared. He was strangled with a ligature and buried in the crawl space.

Gacy not only was a rapist and murderer, he enjoyed torture and sadism. Such was the case during his abduction of Robert Donnelly on December 30, 1977. The youth was taken by Gacy from a Chicago bus stop at gunpoint. Gacy drove him home and raped him, then tortured him over and over with many different devices. Gacy repeatedly dunked the youth's head in a bathtub, reviving him every time he passed out. Donnelly eventually pleaded with Gacy to just put him out of his misery and "get it over with," to which Gacy answered, "I'm getting round to it." Gacy continued the torture and assaults for hours. Once he was done, Gacy removed the handcuffs from his wrists, drove Donnelly back to his place of work, gave him some money, and released him. Despite the young man reporting it to the police, his pleas were in vain: Gacy was questioned on January 6, 1978, and after admitting he had had consensual "slave-sex" with Donnelly, he was let go with no charges at all. Just a month later, as if to further laugh in the face of authority, Gacy killed a 19-year-old named William

Kindred, after abducting him on the way to a bar. Kindred had the twisted honor to be the last victim buried in Gacy's infamous crawl space.

On the 22nd of March, 1978, Gacy stopped his car beside a 26-year-old named Jeffrey Rignall, a young man that wanted to enjoy himself in a bar and have a drink. Gacy offered him a ride to any of the high class bars in the city, and the man, used to hitch-hiking and unsuspecting of the obese friendly man who sat before him, agreed. Gacy suddenly attacked him in the car, forcing a chloroform-laced cloth over his airways. The next thing Rignall remembered was waking up at Gacy's home, manacled, with a naked Gacy standing before him with his torture instruments, describing the effects that each device could cause on the body. Rignall confirmed Gacy's words in practice, as he was raped and tortured for hours; Gacy used lit candles, whips, and other instruments. He was kept in a state between consciousness and unconsciousness by constant application of chloroform. Rignall awoke, dressed, in Lincoln Park, barely alive. From there, he struggled to his girlfriend's apartment. He reported the attack to the police, but Gacy was not investigated. Rignall later received the unfortunate news that the excessive use of chloroform on his body had severely and permanently damaged his liver. Rignall took his opportunity for justice, remembering the model of Gacy's car and nearby streets. He staked out an exit of the highway he had remembered passing and spotted Gacy's black

Oldsmobile in April 1978. Rignall, accompanied by his friends, followed Gacy to 8213 West Summerdale, and he managed to convince police to issue an arrest warrant for battery.

Gacy, meanwhile, was having issues with the lack of room in his crawl space, and considered the attic but decided against it; the leaking from the corpses would damage the home. He instead decided to dispose of his victims by throwing them off the I-55 Bridge into the Des Plaines River. Five bodies were stated by Gacy himself to have been thrown off the bridge, though only four were found. The first victim thrown from the bridge was 20-year-old Timothy O'Rourke, who was killed in mid-June of 1978. His body was found downstream on June 30. The next victim was murdered four months later, a 19-year-old named Frank Landigin. His body was found in the river on November 12. Three weeks later, Gacy killed James Mazzara, a 20-year-old, by strangling him. As for Landigin, Gacy killed him by suffocating him with his own underwear, lodging it down his throat and causing him to drown in his own vomit.

Despite all of the luck that he had enjoyed over the years, law enforcement was a few months away from making his life a living hell. John "Pogo the Clown" Gacy was about to step on thin ice in December of 1978, when he committed his last kidnapping, suffering the same excessive confidence that many serial killers do, once they've murdered enough people without getting caught...

Part 3

Downfall

December 11, 1978.

The date John Wayne Gacy made the mistake that would put him in prison, and sit him on the chair where he would be executed.

Gacy visited a pharmacy in Des Plaines, having been contacted by the owner for a possible remodeling. While discussing the plans, a 15-year-old employee called Robert Jerome Piest overheard Gacy say that his firm hired teenage boys for construction work. Gacy left the store, and Piest proudly told his mother that a contractor was interested in talking to him about a job. He left the store, promising he would return quickly. He failed to keep his promise, and his worried parents filed a missing person report with the police. The owner of the pharmacy mentioned Gacy as the possible contractor involved.

The next evening, Gacy was visited by the police for questioning at his home. He denied talking to Piest, admitting however that he had talked to one of the two employees, only to ask if they had any remodeling materials in the store. He also denied offering jobs to any employees, and promised to go to the station to make an official statement after attending his recently deceased uncle's funeral.

He showed up at the police station at 3:20 am, covered in mud, claiming he had been in a car accident. The police were suspicious. Gacy returned to the station later on and denied being involved in Piest's disappearance. He was asked why he had returned to the pharmacy at 8 p.m. on December 11, and replied he had done so because the owner had called him, reminding him that he had forgotten his appointment book at the store. Unbeknownst to our lying murderer, the police had already spoken to Phil Torf, the pharmacy owner, who stated he had not talked again with Gacy after he left the store.

The Des Plaines police department was unconvinced by Gacy's story, and checked his record. This was the beginning of the end for Gacy. The police discovered the outstanding battery charge against him in Chicago (the one involving Rignall), and his prison sentence in Iowa for sodomy. A judge ordered a search of Gacy's house on December 13, which led to the discovery of several incriminating pieces of evidence: A 1975 high school ring engraved with the initials J.A.S, drivers licenses with many identities, handcuffs, books on homosexuality and pederasty, a syringe, male clothing that didn't belong to Gacy, a 6mm Brevettata starter pistol, and a receipt from the pharmacy where Piest worked. Police assigned two two-man surveillance teams on Gacy while they continued to investigate him regarding Robert Piest's disappearance.

Their investigations led them to discover more details. On December 15, they found the report filed by Jeffrey Rignall, detailing the accusation that Gacy had lured him into his car, used chloroform on him, then raped and dumped him in Lincoln Park with severe chest and facial burns, rectal bleeding, as well as liver damage. After interviewing Gacy's ex-wife, they also learned of John Butkovich's disappearance. Further investigation the same day led them to find the ring belonging to John A. Szyc. Szyc's mother detailed the other items that had gone missing, such as a portable TV set, and that the boy had sold his Plymouth Satellite to a John Gacy. The police confirmed that the Plymouth Satellite was the same one that one of Gacy's employees, Michael Rossi, was now driving.

The next day, Gacy tried to befriend his surveillance detectives, inviting them to restaurants or taking them for drinks in bars or at his home. He denied any involvement in Piest's disappearance, accusing the officers of harassment. He insisted that they were trying to take him down because of his political connections or because they knew he used recreational drugs. He took advantage of his importance to the investigation, and knowing he would not be arrested, he sped away from his surveillance team on more than one occasion, breaking many traffic laws in order to lose them.

Michael Rossi was formally interviewed by investigators on December 17, and gave them the details regarding his purchase of Szyc's car. This didn't lead the investigators any closer to the crimes, but they continued to investigate. When they further examined Gacy's Oldsmobile, they discovered fibers that were similar to human hair, which they sent back to the station for further analysis. Using German Shepherds trained for searching, they let the animals examine each of Gacy's vehicles. The irony arrived in that - despite so many police officers having encountered a chance to capture Gacy - the best clue came from one of the police dogs, which sat down in Gacy's Oldmobile and made a "death reaction," which the dog handler informed was a sign of Piest's body having laid on the car seat. Gacy remained steady, though his patience was beginning to fray, as he spoke with the investigators that night and the next morning, telling them about his activities as a clown. At one point, he told the detectives that clowns were more likely to get away with murder.

Investigators noted how he looked tired and anxious, regularly unshaven and in a drunken state. Gacy decided to make a move that could save him if he pulled it off: driving to his lawyer's office on December 18 to prepare a $750,000 civil suit against the Des Plaines police. While Gacy was at the office, the police were making an important discovery: the pharmacy receipt found among Gacy's belongings was traced to an employee named Kim Byers, who had worked with Piest before he had gone missing. She was contacted and admitted to placing the receipt in a jacket she had given Piest before he left the store with a contractor. This discovery led the police to realize Gacy had lied about having no further contact with Robert Piest after seeing him at the pharmacy on December 11.

Michael Rossi was interviewed again that same evening in an attempt to get him to release more information, and he did, telling police that he had been ordered to spread ten bags of lime in the crawl space by Gacy in 1977. Investigators knew they were cornering their suspect, and believed that many, if not all, of the clues lay at Gacy's home.

On December 19, both sides played their cards. Gacy filed the civil suit against the Des Plaines police, and investigators compiled evidence for a second search warrant of Gacy's house. Gacy invited two of the surveillance detectives into his home, and as one officer distracted him with conversation, the other walked into Gacy's bedroom in an attempt to match the serial number on the portable television to the one stolen from John Szyc, but he was unsuccessful. However, while flushing the bathroom toilet, he smelled an odor similar to rotting corpses coming from a heating duct.

David Cram (The ex-Army lad who had escaped the handcuff trick) and Michael Rossi were interviewed on December 20. Both of them hammered the metaphorical nails into Gacy's coffin; Michael Rossi was interrogated until the breaking point, when he admitted Piest's body had probably been placed in the crawl space. While taking a polygraph test, he nervously told police about trenches he had dug in the crawl space at Gacy's insistence. Cram, still unforgiving of what Gacy had done to him, informed the police of Gacy's attempts to rape him in 1976, and talked of Gacy's nerves at suspecting the first search of his home had lead the investigators to find something in the crawl space. He himself had dug trenches for Gacy in the crawl space, having been told they were for plumbing. However, their dimensions--two feet wide, six feet long and two feet deep--were the size of graves.

Sam Amirante, Gacy's lawyer, received his client on the evening of December 20. Gacy was disheveled and asked for a drink immediately, and Amirante gave him a bottle of whiskey. The lawyer asked Gacy what he was there to talk about, and Gacy told him the boy on the front page of the newspaper on his desk, Robert Piest, was dead, his body in a river. He began to confess; the entire confession took hours, lasting into the following morning. He talked about being "the judge, jury and executioner of many, many people," and talked about some of his victims by name, while others were referred to as "male prostitutes" and "liars." He specifically gave the location of their corpses as his crawl space, while a few others had been thrown into the Des Plaines River. He talked about the method of killing, though he also spoke of having woken up to find "dead, strangled kids" on his floor, as if he had not been the one to kill them. He then went on to admit he had killed a crying Piest with a tourniquet, before falling asleep halfway through the confession. Several hours later, he woke up, and when asked by Amirante whether he remembered confessing to killing around 30 people earlier that morning, he dismissively shook his head and left the office, ignoring Amirante's offers of advice.

Gacy's last day of freedom was a desperate day for him. He knew his arrest was inevitable, and only wished to say his farewells to his friends before he was put away for a long time. The first thing he did after leaving the lawyer's office was drive to a Shell gas station, where he gave a small bag of cannabis to the attendant, who immediately handed the bag to the surveillance officers. The attendant told the police that Gacy had spoken to him, saying "The end is coming. These guys are going to kill me." Gacy then drove to a fellow contractor, Ronald Rhode's, home. Once in the living room, he hugged the man, while telling him he had "killed thirty people, give or take a few." Gacy drove his way to meet with Michael Rossi and David Cram, surveillance officers noting he was praying with a rosary while driving. He talked to both Cram and Rossi at Cram's home, then had Cram drive him to meet with Leroy Stevens, his lawyer. As they spoke, Cram informed the officers that Gacy had confessed to both him and his lawyers his guilt in over thirty murders. Gacy finished his meeting and requested Cram take him to Maryhill Cemetery, where his father was buried.

Gacy continued to travel to various locations, but the police decided to arrest him on charges of possession and distribution of marijuana, fearing his behavior would lead him to commit suicide before they could arrest him for the murders. A search warrant was issued at 4:30 pm, December 21, one day before Gacy's civil suit hearing was set to occur, with the specific purpose of searching Gacy's crawl space for Robert Piest's body. Police and evidence technicians flew to Gacy's home, finally standing before the key to the investigation. Gacy's final attempt at dissuading authorities had been to flood the crawl space with water, but the police simply replaced the sump pump's plug and waited for the water to drain. A technician named Daniel Genty entered the crawl space, and started digging. Minutes later, he encountered a gruesome discovery: putrefied flesh and a human arm bone. Turning, he called up to his fellow investigators. They could now charge Gacy with murder.

Gacy confessed in the early hours of December 22, knowing his arrest was inevitable. He admitted that since 1972 he had committed around 25 to 30 murders, all of whom were, according to him, teenage male runaways or male prostitutes that he abducted from Chicago's Greyhound Bus station, Bughouse Square, or off the city streets. He would grab them by force or con them into his car, posing as a sheriff on many occasions, and then they would be driven back to Gacy's house with the promise of a job or the offer of money for sex.

He further admitted that once they were at his home, he would handcuff or bind them, then choke them with a rope or board as he sexually assaulted them. He used cloth rags or clothing to muffle their screams. He also talked about the tourniquet, or "rope trick" in Gacy's own words. He admitted to having been inspired by reading about the Houston Mass Murders, a series of killings in which three men had restrained their victims (also young boys) while sexually abusing and torturing before murdering them.

Gacy spoke of killing mostly lonely victims, though he had killed two victims on the same night on at least three occasions, and told the detectives he would store the victim's bodies under his bed for up to 24 hours before burying them, sometimes even embalming them in his garage prior to burial. He would pour quicklime to hasten the decomposition of the bodies, and admitted he had been weeks away from completely covering the crawl space with concrete in January 1979. He had lost count of the number of victims buried in his crawl space and admitted five victims had been thrown into the Des Plaines River after reconsidering using the attic.

He finally confessed to Robert Piest's death, telling them he had strangled the youth on December 11, then slept beside the youth's body that evening before throwing it into the river. The car accident he claimed to have been in, *had* actually happened, Gacy suffering a minor traffic accident after disposing of Piest's body. Gacy drew a diagram of his basement and home to help the detectives find all the bodies.

He accompanied the police back to his home on December 22 to show them where he had buried Butkovitch's body, and then led them to the location on the I-55 Bridge where he had thrown the body of Piest and four other victims. Between that date and December 28, 27 bodies were discovered at Gacy's home. Excavations began in March 1979, despite Gacy's insistence that all bodies had been found. He was wrong, either intentionally or not, and on March 9, a

28th victim was found, close to a barbecue grill pit in the backyard. One week later, another body was found beneath the joists of the dining room floor. A total of 29 bodies were found, and in April 1979, Gacy's house was demolished.

The bodies that were dug from under Gacy's home were found to have been killed in numerous ways that varied in their horrifying nature. Some of them had plastic bags over their heads or upper torsos to avoid leaking of blood, others still had ligatures around their necks. Some others were found with cloth gags lodged deep down their throats, meaning they had died of asphyxiation, not of strangulation. In some more horrible cases, prescription bottles and other objects were found lodged in the corpse's anus. All of the bodies were in advanced state of decomposition and required dental records to be identified.

However, to this day, even with the technology we've invented since the '70s, seven victims have never been identified. Robert Piest's corpse was found on April 9, 1979, entangled in exposed roots on the edge of the Des Plaines River. Paper-like material was found shoved down his throat; he had been asphyxiated.

Part 4

Aftermath & End

John Wayne Gacy's trial began on February 3, 1980, and he was charged with 33 murders. It took place in Cook County, Illinois. Gacy spent a year with doctors at the Menard Correctional Center, undergoing psychological tests before a panel of psychiatrists. They were to determine whether he was mentally fit to stand trial.

Gacy believed that he shared his body with multiple personalities, suffering from the disorder of the same name. His defense attempted to plead not guilty by reason of insanity, and among those in his defense were three experts who found Gacy to be a paranoid schizophrenic who suffered from a multiple personality disorder.

The prosecutors alleged that Gacy was fully sane and aware of his actions, citing several events where he had acted with premeditation, and the way he had manipulated the truth many times to avoid detection and capture. Doctors also refuted Gacy's defense of multiple personality disorder and insanity. Two PDM employees testified against him, confessing Gacy had made them dig trenches in the crawl space. David Cram himself testified against Gacy, stating that he had been contracted to dig a drainage trench in a marked location beneath the house where bodies had been found. Michael Rossi testified immediately after, showing where he had dug a trench of his own. He spoke of how Gacy would periodically check on them to make sure they did not dig anywhere not marked by the sticks Gacy had placed.

On February 18, Cook County's medical examiner came forward to give a report on the recovery of remains, stating that thirteen victims had died of asphyxiation; six had died of ligature strangulation and one of multiple stab wounds to the chest. Ten other victims found had undetermined causes of death, but were also ruled as homicides. Gacy's defense team desperately claimed the possibility that all 33 murders were accidental erotic asphyxia deaths, which was a laughable and disrespectful disaster of allegations, but as expected, it was countered by the overwhelming evidence.

The next people to testify against Gacy would overwhelmingly decide the outcome of the trial: Jeffrey Rignall, David Voorhees, and Robert Donnelly. Rignall told the court all of the terrible things done to him, detailing the assaults and torture he suffered while abducted. He wept many times while telling his story, and vomited when a doctor cross-examined his case.

Donald Voorhees, the one Gacy had sexually assaulted back in 1967 and who had put Gacy in prison, came forth to tell the court how Gacy had tried to stop Voorhees from testifying the first time by hiring someone to assault and spray him in the face with Mace. A week later, Donnelly testified, also recounting his ordeal. He showed great signs of distress - almost breaking down on several occasions - and Gacy himself laughed while Donnelly spoke, but to the youth's credit, he finished his testimony.

Eventually, the final arguments began, and the Prosecuting Attorney, Terry Sullivan, stated: "John Gacy has accounted for more human devastation than many earthly catastrophes, but one must tremble. I tremble when thinking about just how close he came to getting away with it all," as well as calling Voorhees and Donnelly "living dead" for the traumas Gacy had left them with. Sam Amirante attempted to protect his client, saying Sullivan's arguments had aroused hatred against Gacy, and portraying Gacy as a man who acted without control of his actions. The prosecutors showed photographs of Gacy's identified victims, asking for the jury to show justice, not sympathy, since Gacy had shown none himself.

It was finally in March, 1980, when the jury decided the sentence. Gacy was sentenced to death for the twelve counts of murder upon which the prosecution had sought this penalty, and twenty one natural life sentences. An initial date of execution was set for June 2, 1980.

Gacy was transferred to Menard Correctional Center in Chester, Illinois, where he remained on death row for 14 years. He took up painting while in prison, clowns being the main theme, even including himself as "Pogo the Clown" in many works. These works were eventually auctioned for prices as high as $20,000 each, some of them bought by a victim's family for the sole reason to be destroyed. Galleries can still be found online.

Despite many appeals and opposition, the Illinois Supreme Court finally set an execution date: May 10, 1994. Gacy was transferred to Statesville Correctional Center. He was allowed a private picnic on the prison grounds with his family. His last meal consisted of a dozen deep fried shrimp, a bucket of original recipe chicken from KFC, a pound of fresh strawberries and French fries. Gacy showed no remorse until the last minute, telling his lawyer that killing him would not compensate for what he had done, nor would it bring his victims back. His last spoken words became infamous: **"Kiss my ass."**

Despite a short delay when the chemicals to be used clogged the IV tube, the execution took place by lethal injection. Eighteen minutes later, at 12:58 a.m., May 10, 1994, Gacy was dead. His brain was removed after his death and after an examination, revealed no abnormalities, despite the defense's allegations.

Conclusion

The monster was dead.

The story ended for him, but not for his living victims, or his murdered victims' families. Only 25 of his victims were ever identified. As recently as 2013, investigations continued to try and identify the remaining victims.

To this day, there remain strong theories on Gacy having accomplices who helped him abduct and murder youths. In fact, after his arrest, Gacy asked if any of his "associates" had also been arrested. When questioned if those associates had participated directly or indirectly, Gacy replied, "Directly." He stated that two or three employees had assisted him in his murders, and Rignall himself spoke of waking up during his prolonged torture to see a young, brown-haired man kneeling before him and watching his torture. Gacy himself claimed that he had not been present in Chicago during many of the disappearances. Amirante himself cryptically said that Gacy once stated "There is a picture of all my victims, together. I look at the pictures and have no memory of any of them."

Despite this evidence, no one else was ever charged for the murders, so perhaps there was a darker side of PDM, one that continued operating even as Gacy was on death row.

Maybe they still operate to this day, in the shadows...

* * *

And so, the story ends, and we hope you have enjoyed reading about the case of the Killer Clown, **John Wayne Gacy**. If there has been a lesson learned from all of this, it could be: <u>NEVER TRUST A CLOWN</u>!

Thanks again for downloading this book!